If I Really Believe, Why Do I Have These Doubts?

FOREWORD BY BILL HYBELS

If I Really Believe, Why Do I Have These Doubts?

Revised and Updated

Discussion Questions Included

Dr. Lynn Anderson

HOWARD
PUBLISHING CO.

Our purpose at Howard Publishing is to:

- *Increase faith* in the hearts of growing Christians
- *Inspire holiness* in the lives of believers
- *Instill hope* in the hearts of struggling people everywhere

Because He's coming again!

Published by Howard Publishing Co., Inc.,
3117 North 7th Street, West Monroe, Louisiana 71291-2227

00 01 02 03 04 05 06 07 08 09   10 9 8 7 6 5 4 3 2 1

Library of Congress Cataloging-in-Publication Data
Anderson, Lynn, 1936–
    If I really believe, why do I have these doubts? : overcoming obstacles to faith / Lynn Anderson.— Rev. and updated.
       p. cm.
    Includes bibliographical references.
    ISBN 1-58229-117-9
    1. Faith. I. Title.

BV4637 .A63 2000
234'.23—dc21   00-026321

The quote on page 172 is excerpted from "The Family Reunion" in *The Family Reunion,* copyright 1939 by T. S. Eliot and renewed 1967 by Esme Valerie Eliot. It is reprinted by permission of Harcourt Brace Jovanovich, Inc.

Scripture quotations not otherwise marked are from the Holy Bible, New International Version. Copyright © 1973, 1978, 1984 International Bible Society. Used by permission of Zondervan Bible Publishers. All rights reserved. Other Scriptures are quoted from The Holy Bible, Authorized King James Version (KJV), © 1961 by the National Publishing Co.; and The Holy Bible, New King James Version (NKJV), © 1982 by Thomas Nelson, Inc.

Edited by Anne Christian Buchanan
Interior design by Stephanie Denney
Discussion questions by John Ogren

What Goes Into the Mind
Comes Out in a Life™

To my parents
Lawrence and Mary Anderson
now gone home
through whom I received faith

and to my wife
Carolyn
who follows faith's winding road beside me

and to our children
Michele, Deborah, Jon, and Christopher
who live by faith

and to our grandchildren.

"Oh, may all who come behind us find us faithful."

CONTENTS

FOREWORD

One day a senior-level staff person slipped into my office, fought back tears, and with a tremor in his voice admitted that he was sinking into seas of doubt—serious doubts about his faith and the Founder of it. I quietly listened and later assured him that I could identify with his plight.

It wasn't the first time something like this had happened, and I know it won't be the last. But from now on I will have more than an understanding spirit to offer my wavering visitors.

If I Really Believe, Why Do I Have These Doubts? is Lynn Anderson at his best. The subject matter he delves into demands both intellectual and emotional honesty, and Lynn delivers on both counts. My faith was bolstered through reading this book, and I have no doubt yours will be too.

Bill Hybels
Senior Pastor
Willow Creek Community Church

ACKNOWLEDGMENTS

This book is not theoretical. It is not meant to be merely a good read. Rather, it is a slice of real life. Years before any words arrived on paper, this book was forming out of my own personal struggle to deal with doubt and find faith. It grew as other doubters shared their stories with me. The shape of the book was hammered out during numerous classes, seminars, and retreats I have led under the title "I Believe, But..." Hundreds of bull sessions after these presentations have honed and expanded my thoughts.

This means, of course, that I am indebted to more people than I can possibly remember, much less list here. But special appreciation goes to some closest to mind.

First, I am indebted to a crowd of writers whose works have helped me through tough times and have influenced these pages. Most of these are credited in text or endnote. Some names have long since fled my consciousness, although your insights still shape me and may even be confused with my own.

Most of the people stories in this book are real and have been told to me by the individuals who actually lived them. However, I have combined some stories with others, assigned fictitious names, and shuffled places, genders, and even plots to protect confidences so that any identifiable "similarities to persons living or dead" are purely coincidental. Nevertheless, I am indebted to these people. In fact, I wish some could be named; they are the real heroes of this book.

Special thanks to Patsy Strader for tireless typing and to Lyn Rose for her endless hours at the word processor and at the library digging up buried footnotes.

Kudos also to Charette Barna, who cheered me by mail, coached me by phone, and prayed my spirits up and out. Thanks also to my line editor, Anne Christian Buchanan, who stuck with me through the painstaking process of fine-tuning the manuscript and helped me feel confident that I was saying what I wanted to say.

Thanks also to the staff and elders of the Preston Road Church of Christ, who patiently allowed me to spend the necessary hours to wrap up this book when I had been on board as their pulpit minister only a few short months.

And thanks to a supportive family who believes in me and in this book enough to "do without much Dad" at times.

Most of all, I am grateful to you, my loving and patient Lord. You have never left me nor forsaken me, even when I was angry at you or wasn't sure I believed in you or broke your heart. And Lord, as another doubter picks up this book, may the thoughts on these pages help and comfort that soul as they are helping and comforting me.

You are my life, my light, and my salvation. I love you, trust you, and praise you.

And Lord, I do believe…please help my unbelief!

I Believe,
But...

His name is forgotten. Let's call him Ketar, which in Hebrew means to solve a problem or to resolve doubt...

Ketar's fingers twitched and trembled, but his arm lay warm and gentle around the wet shoulders of his sullen son. Years of fear and frustration choked his voice. With the side of his thumb, Ketar brushed tears from the corners of his eyes.

The terror had struck again. Once more his boy had been dragged from near drowning. The young man's soaked clothing clung to his shivering body but did not cover the burn scars networking his back.

"Sometimes the demon throws him into the water, sometimes into the fire," Ketar anguished as he stood in front of the carpenter's son. "If you can do anything..."

"*If* I can?" Jesus responded. "All things are possible to those who believe."

"Believe? I do."

But in reality, what little faith Ketar possessed didn't seem to connect with his life. How does one believe? He had often prayed for the boy, but nothing changed. Had he really expected it would? His long days and dark nights seemed all the same. He was running out of hope.

His son was not the only one who desperately needed help. Ketar needed it himself! He could find no clear prism for separating the dark demonic forces from the light of heaven.

"I do believe," he murmured, "but…"

Could there be hope? Maybe the carpenter's son could restore balance to his world and still the voices of its demons.

"I do believe, but…help me. Help me overcome my *unbelief…*

my unbelief…

my unbelief…"[1]

Although Ketar's words fell only softly, twenty centuries ago, their echo has not died! Some believers still wrestle with doubts today.

And help—real help—is still available!

PART 1

If I Believe, Why Do I Feel This Way?

In the middle of the journey of our life,
I came to myself in a dark wood
where the straightway was lost.
—DANTE

When Faith Goes Flat

A friend of mine in Houston opened his mail, and out tumbled this troubling letter:

Dear —,

Something has been bothering me of late, which I think merits mentioning to you. I've lost God. I can no longer find Him in my life. This is no case of sophomoric atheism, but rather a matter-of-fact statement—in the same way, for example, that I might say, "I misplaced my car keys."

I'm not denying God's existence at all. But for me, He simply is not real.

This fact became apparent to me the other night when I tried to pray. About three sentences into it, I realized I wasn't really feeling what I was saying, and probably God wasn't hearing me, anyway. The very act of prayer suddenly became tragically absurd. So I shut up, took two aspirin, and went to sleep.

But the issue has been haunting me off and on ever since. I know one response for this kind of statement is to say God exists in people and we should look for Him there. Well, I'll buy that. But what has become of the transcendent Deity? To whom do I pray? Where's that personal Lord and Savior of yore? If you've any thoughts on this subject, I'd like to hear them.

This letter grabbed my attention because, in many ways, I readily identify with its writer. I also identify—deeply—with Ketar, our worried friend who begged Jesus for help with his faltering faith. In fact, one reason I am writing this book is that I do believe but still need help for my unbelief.

You may have doubts too. They may take the form of powerful, painful questions about God's love or God's power or even God's existence. Or they may emerge as vague, unexpressed feelings of dissatisfaction and disappointment—a nagging sense that your once-vital and fully rounded faith has gone flat as an old tire.

Your doubts may be huge boulders that block the road to Christian commitment. Or they may be little rocks in your shoe, bothersome little distractions that sap some of your spiritual energy and keep you from finding full, wholehearted joy in your Christian walk. Either way, I suspect your doubts are what prodded you to open this book. Maybe you resonate with the old Gordon Lightfoot song: "I don't know where we went wrong, but the feeling's gone and I just can't get it back."[1] Somewhere in your mind and heart lurk questions such as these:

- Is God really out there?
- If so, does He really care about me?
- Does anything really change when I pray and study the Bible?
- Why don't I feel as I used to feel about my faith?
- If I really believe, why do I have all these nagging doubts?

And that's the second reason I am writing—to connect with your doubts.

In the years since I first summoned the courage to speak honestly and openly about my faith struggles, all sorts of people have come out of the woodwork—many of them conscientious, church-going people—and told me, "I feel that way too." They seem relieved that someone like me—a minister, a former missionary, someone who has followed a Christian vocation all his life—still finds faith a struggle at times. And they seem encouraged that, despite my ongoing doubts, I haven't given up on the faith journey.

So let me begin by relating a little of my own story—the story of one who has struggled with doubt since early childhood. It may not be just like your story, but I hope it will give you permission to go back through your own experience and think honestly about how your doubts feel to you.

CONFESSIONS OF A ROCK KICKER

The white rubber toes of my black canvas sneakers carried fresh grass stains and scuffs from kicking rocks. The snow was finally gone, new green spread softly across the rolling Canadian prairies, and crocuses bloomed on the hillsides. For most twelve-year-old country boys, the two-mile walk home from school on a warm spring afternoon would have been a sheer delight—but not for me. While my lowered eyes watched the toes of my sneakers and the rock I was kicking down the road, my restless mind tumbled and wrestled through a labyrinth of brooding thoughts.

"Why have I never seen God?" I mused. "I talk to Him, but He never talks to me. All last year I begged Him for a bicycle, but I never got one. Is there really any reason to believe in God? Or do people just pretend there is a God in order to frighten each other into being good? If there really is a God, He sure seems far away.

"But then…everyone loves my dad, and he believes in God. Could he be wrong?"

My father actually homesteaded land in Canada, and he farmed over half of his life. Six grades measured his formal schooling, but not his learning. Until his death at age eighty-five, he read voraciously. He had the soul of a poet—and a winsome, authentic faith that led people to respect and trust him.

Dad seemed to see the Almighty everywhere.

After supper, on many frosty winter evenings, Dad and I pulled on our parkas, mittens, and overshoes and trudged to the barn to finish a few chores. I recall how one night, as the hard, dry snow scrunched under our boots and the soft light of the lantern spilled across the whiteness, Dad stopped and pointed to the bright particles glistening at the rim of our pool of light. "Look how rich we are," he reminded me. "God has scattered diamonds on our path."

Late one spring, as two storm fronts met over our farm at sunset, the sky displayed an awesome extravaganza of color and motion. Dad took off his cap and stood transfixed as if in worship with the swirling colors reflected in his eyes. Then he pulled me close and talked quietly of the power and majesty of God.

During the long, bitter Saskatchewan winters, our house was heated by an ornate, glass-windowed, coal-devouring heater. A brief moment of one long-ago winter night still stands vividly in my memory. Deep in the night, I heard movement nearby and sleepily opened one eye. The glow from the heater, the only light in the room, danced across Dad's rounded shoulders and his tousled head. In his longhandles, with the funny rump-line, Dad was kneeling by my bed in prayer.

My father possessed the purest heart and most steadfast faith of any man I ever knew. I loved him and respected him deeply. But somehow, I couldn't seem to feel the things I sensed he felt. As I kicked rocks down the road, I would think, "Daddy would be so disappointed in me if he knew that I don't really for sure believe in God. Will I ever believe *for sure?* Or will I always wonder?"

But the fabric of my doubt was not cut with a clean edge. Interspersed between periods of kicking rocks were times when God seemed intensely real.

The year I turned thirteen, I rode horseback five miles to school each day. Sometimes this meant riding alone through stormy weather and arriving home after dusk. God became a frightened boy's comfort then. More than once, I now recall, faith dispelled anxiety and loneliness. To the jerky rhythm of my plodding black mare, through swirling snow and gathering darkness, my child's voice, half whispering, half singing, often mingled with the prairie wind:

He leadeth me! O blessed tho't!
O words with heav'nly comfort fraught!
Whate'er I do, where'er I be,
Still 'tis God's hand that leadeth me.[2]

In those moments, God seemed not only real but near and personal, lifting my spirits and warming my lonely places. I savored those feelings, sometimes for days. Years later I would long for their return. For in the years that followed, I continued to kick the rocks of doubt ahead of me. My doubting changed shape over time, but it never completely went away.

My childhood uncertainty grew into an adolescent fear that I could never measure up to God's standards, which in turn was fed by a college student's intellectual quest and a young man's spiritual searching. Even though I chose to enter the ministry and even became a missionary for a time, I often felt like a fraud, because I wasn't sure I myself had bought into what I was "selling." For much of my life I have been haunted by feelings of guilt, hopelessness, and fear—all stemming from these fundamental doubts.

For much of my life I have been haunted by feelings of guilt, hopelessness, and fear—all stemming from these fundamental doubts.

From time to time I have experienced special moments, when God seemed intensely real—when I could almost physically feel a "presence." But those special experiences wouldn't last long, nor could they be recaptured at will. Sometimes they seemed like brief moments of faith against a backdrop of ongoing doubt.

But don't let me leave you in these dark, haunted chambers, Yes, I have been a periodic doubter all of my life. But life is different for me now—vastly different—than it was in those painful days.

And no, the doubts haven't all disappeared. In fact, sometimes they still come thick and fast, from unexpected directions and with formidable power, presenting surprising new profiles. But I view my doubts differently now, and they don't torment me the way they used to.

I have not arrived. I don't really expect to. But that's okay, because I have learned that finding faith is not so much like finding a parking place as it is like discovering a winding road—and I *am* on the road. As a believer coming to terms with my doubts, I have chosen to follow the trail of faith (in spite of a few rocks in the road), trusting each day to the best light I have. And I do not intend to turn back.

THE MANY FACES OF DOUBT

Possibly you identify in some way with my pilgrimage. Even now you may be wandering in some dark haunted woods of doubt, wondering whether God is really there at all. I have met many a fellow traveler in these shadowy places.

One pilgrim was a business executive, accustomed to having his orders carried out on the spot. His doubts multiplied when confronted with God's apparent silence. He blustered, "If I were God I would show people who was boss."

That man could well have been the little boy in the cartoon who was down on his knees by the bedside, saying his prayers, almost out of patience with the Almighty: "Aunt Stella isn't married yet. Uncle Hubert hasn't got a job. Daddy's hair is still falling out. I'm tired of saying prayers for this family without getting results."[3]

This silence in the sky, this waiting around for something to happen that never does, can be quite serious. You soon discover that life is often full of this waiting—and full of sad or angry people wondering why. Vice triumphs over virtue, things go terribly wrong, good people get killed or knocked around, the heavens don't open to destroy the wicked, evil people laugh in the face of God, the world rolls on, and nothing changes.

William Blake seems to understand the pain of this kind of doubt in *The Marriage of Heaven and Hell:*

Down the winding cavern we groped our tedious way till a void boundless as the nether sky appeared beneath us, and we held on by the roots of trees and hung over this immensity, but I said: "If you please, we will commit ourselves to this void, and see whether Providence is here also."[4]

Those of us whose doubt stares at the silent sky or hangs over a void sometimes find ourselves wondering, "Is anyone really here?"

But that may not be your problem at all.

You may be thinking, "Yes, I am a doubter too," but you can't seem to connect with my story or with the impatient executive or with Blake. That's not surprising. Countless conversations across the years have convinced me that doubt comes in many shapes and sizes, and my size may not fit you at all.

You may not be a minister, for example, but a CEO or homemaker or farmer or student or accountant or physician. Your disposition may not match mine either. And your doubts may have an entirely different feel to them.

You may relate to Eric, whose doubting was more like wandering through a dry, dusty landscape than struggling through a dark wood.

Eric grew up in a Christian family. Christ stood at the center of Eric's world during high-school days. After graduating from a prestigious university, Eric landed a teaching job in a top-flight high school. But now Eric was at mid-career. He loved his work, but the pressure of the secular environment had relentlessly eroded many of his feelings about God. And although he remained active in his church, he gradually felt his faith sliding down his relevancy scale.

Eric's voice sounded tired, almost cold, when he described his reaction to a public Scripture reading:

That impersonal voice reading from the King James Bible seemed so irrelevant. I was neither moved by it nor ashamed of it. It just felt bizarre, antiquated language. Ideas that seemed disconnected from any realities around me. I felt as if that mechanical reading voice were trying to converse with a person inside me who had already died. It wasn't as if I decided not to believe it anymore. Just that somehow it didn't connect—and I didn't care.

Eric said he had begun to feel that worship was an absurd routine at best. He was bored with the same old paths through religion and the lingo that went with it. He longed to be grabbed by some new gusto because, to him, "The Christian tradition crackles with dryness and sterility. The whole business of believing seems either deadly dull or impossible to achieve very well—at least by me."

Or maybe you would understand Louise better. Louise called herself a doubter too, but doubt felt different for her than it did for Eric and me. Louise's doubt was interlaced with guilt and fear:

> James and I slept together quite awhile before we got married. This violated major rules for both of us, but rules didn't seem to matter then. Now, we've been married four years, and we are overwhelmed by a flood of guilt that interferes with everything —even our sex life! Is God punishing us? Intellectually I know God forgives, but I chose to turn my back on Him for so long, how could He accept *me*? In fact, I can't even remember a lot of simple things about Jesus that I knew before I quit church. How can God still like me?

Then again, these examples may seem a little too extreme for you to relate to. You would never use words like *bizarre, absurd, dull,* or *impossible* about your religious tradition, and you aren't racked by guilt over turning your back on God. In fact, you may care deeply about your faith—it just doesn't seem to be working the way it should. Maybe your doubt feels more like vague dissatisfaction or, to use Philip Yancey's phrase, "disappointment with God."[5] You even hesitate to call it unbelief—but it still bothers you.

"I've been a Christian for years," confessed Carmen, "and church is a big part of my life. But lately—I don't know—I've had a little trouble keeping my mind on God. I sit in the service, but my mind wanders. I teach Sunday school, but mainly because *somebody* has to do it. I try to have a quiet time in the morning, but I keep thinking about what Andy said last night or what I'm doing for lunch—or I fall asleep. I keep telling myself I just need to be more disciplined. But I also keep wondering, 'Is faith supposed to be this hard?'"

Then again, you may be one of those people whose doubt rises out of the crucible of suffering. Rather than creating a sense of distance and disconnectedness or disappointment, your doubt may focus on sharp areas of pain and raise pointed questions.

Deborah certainly had a right to ask those kinds of questions. Two years ago Mark ran off with a much younger woman and left Deborah to raise their three kids on her salary as a secretary. Although Mark claimed some new relationship with the Holy Spirit, he conveniently forgot about child support and alimony payments for months on end. When desperation drove Deborah to beg Mark for financial help, he only chided her "weak faith." Deborah had long since used up all her tears. Her anger and helplessness hardened, leaving only a steely glint in her eyes.

She faced me across the table, but somehow I sensed she was actually contemplating a horizon somewhere miles behind my head: "I don't feel much like talking to God these days. Frankly, for a little while, I don't want much to do with Him. Oh, I'm not going to give up, but, Lynn, could you tell me where is God in all this? I have no idea."

I understand Michael's doubts too. He and Susan both loved their new jobs and good salaries. Three years ago they bought a new house. Their four-year-old son lit up their lives.

Maybe your doubt feels more like vague dissatisfaction. You may even hesitate to call it unbelief—but it still bothers you.

Then came the news of Susan's second pregnancy, and the little family rejoiced. But when Michael came by my office four months later, his chin dragged the floor. There were complications with the pregnancy. Susan had been ordered to bed, which put a quick end to her income. Already, medical bills were piling up. And Michael's company, hit hard by an economic recession, was making severe cutbacks. Michael was shuffled to a different department, his salary cut nearly in half, and the possibility loomed that he would be out of work altogether.

The baby came prematurely and spent six enormously expensive weeks in the hospital. Then there was some problem with Michael and Susan's medical insurance, and they discovered the baby was not covered. Michael and Susan had never made a late payment in their lives, but suddenly they couldn't even manage their house payments, let alone the staggering medical bills. They lost their house and their credit rating. Whenever the doorbell rang, Michael and Susan hid, fearing bill collectors. The mounting pressure was beginning to threaten their marriage.

"A year and a half ago," Michael told me, "I was more excited about God than I ever have been in my life. Right now, I don't even know if He's there. If He is, He sure doesn't care about me. Or if He does, He doesn't seem to be able to do anything.

"Lynn," Michael asked me sadly, "what do you do when you're fresh out of faith?"

"I REALLY WANT TO BELIEVE!"

That question, in a nutshell, is what challenged me to write this book.

What do you do when you're fresh out of faith?

Or, more to the point, what do you do when you *want* a strong, confident, vital faith but for one reason or another you just can't find it?

What can possibly be more disconcerting than to genuinely long for faith but have it continually elude you? Or to sense that your faith in God no longer connects with your day-to-day living.

Regardless of the shape doubt takes or the reason it comes, doubt can torpedo your peace of mind. Your confidence in God can leak out of your belief until faith goes flat. You may keep on following the same religious forms, but you don't really seem to live inside them. Consequently, whatever faith you have left seems only a second-hand religious experience. (As I and many other Christians have discovered, it is possible to know all the stock answers, to go through all the motions of religion, and still feel "fresh out of faith.")

If you cannot get in touch with God, if you lose the ability to trust in Someone bigger than all of this, life turns bland at best and unbearable at worst. We human beings need faith—to give us strength, to give us courage, to give our lives hope and color and meaning. As Cherea says in Camus's *Caligula,*

> To lose one's life is a little thing, and I will have the courage when necessary. But to see the sense of life dissipated, to see our reason for existence disappear; that is what is insupportable. A man cannot live without a reason.[6]

We all long to know that our lives have meaning, that there really is a purpose for our existence. Perhaps for this reason, I have found that most of those who still talk about their doubts, deep down, really want to believe. Of the hundreds of doubters who have opened their lives to me, I cannot remember one who said, "I do not want to believe." There seemed to be a universal will to have faith. Each in his or her own way sounded a lot like Ketar: "I believe, but help..."

For me, this is a crucial distinction. I am convinced that being a doubter is very different from being a nonbeliever. Nonbelievers are people who have made a conscious or unconscious choice not to have faith. Doubters, on the other hand, may not be sure that they have real faith. They may even wish they didn't believe, or they don't know exactly what to believe. But even when they cannot recognize it, they still *want* to have faith.

Before you spend the time it takes to read the rest of this book, you may want to pause and ask yourself, "What do I really want from this book? Do I long for more faith than I have? Or am I actually looking for a way to get rid of whatever faith I do have? What really is important to me?"

If your answer is "I believe, but help my unbelief," keep reading.

YOU ARE NOT ALONE

Most of all, I hope this book convinces you that whatever your experience of doubt, you are not alone.

I have taken the time to tell my story and the stories of others so that you can hear a variety of experiences and perhaps relate to one of them. I hope I have helped you connect with the feelings and experiences of some other doubters.

Many who have "groped this winding cavern" alone for years have never heard anyone talk about such things. Each fears him- or herself to be the only person in the world thinking such unthinkable thoughts and experiencing such bizarre feelings.

I felt that way. For years, through these dark, lonely, and frightening periods of my developing faith, I had not the slightest notion that so many others shared my private hell. Convinced that discussing such things was definitely off limits, I was terrified that somehow my true feelings might get out and I would be ruined. Surely to be so different from people I trusted and loved must either be sick or evil or both.

Paradoxically, I was immobilized by the fear that other professed believers, deep down, were just like me and thus not to be trusted. No wonder I felt alone in my universe.

The fog began to lift for me when I discovered that it was okay to talk about doubts. I gradually learned that admitting my faith struggle does not make doubt worse—as if admitting my doubts would make them come true. Instead, facing up to my doubts somehow opens up the possibility of renewed faith. Now I am convinced, as Os Guinness says, that "the shame is not that people have doubts, but that they are ashamed of them."7

I have also found that admitting my doubts has introduced me to more fellow strugglers than I ever dreamed existed. In recent years, I have begun to talk about these feelings—furtively, privately, secretly at first, then more openly and finally publicly to thousands of people. And every time I speak on this subject, I am overrun at the door by fellow doubters, then besieged with weeks of follow-up letters and phone calls.

Like me, crowds of others walk in the shadows alone, fearing they are "different." And they are profoundly *relieved to* know that they are not alone in their struggle, that other people feel the way they do, and that doubt is not the death knell of faith. It is my prayer that this book will bring you that kind of relief and encouragement—and then provide some practical help for getting your faith back off the ground.

A Look down the Road

This book is for you,

- if you ever wonder about the genuineness of your own faith
- if you wrestle with doubt, either in the form of shattering angst or niggling, unspoken questions
- if your belief doesn't seem to connect with your life
- if you admire the faith of those around you but sometimes wonder if faith is worth the effort

If, like Ketar, you believe but still need help with your unbelief, then take heart. There is a road back to faith.

We have already looked at some of the many forms doubt can take. Next we will consider some of the factors that may shape your experience of doubt. We will block some blind alleys that seem to lead many searchers in disappointing directions. Then we will sharpen our definition of faith so that we will know what we are looking for on the road. We will mark the developmental stages of the faith journey so that you can get a feel for your own progress.

The core of the book will suggest five clear steps to take in order to get your faith journey underway—or get it started again when it has floundered. The book will end not by guiding us into a parking spot, at an arrival point, but by calling us to the unfolding mystery and excitement of a road that winds through faith's heartland.

Let's start our journey by looking at some of the reasons faith may go flat.

Tracing
Your
Tracks

It was March of 1947. I was headed home from school. And even
though the snow was coming down harder than I had ever seen in
my eleven years, I walked out into the blizzard with confidence.

After all these years, I still can't believe how quickly and completely I lost the trail—or what it took to get me back on track.

All morning the skies had grown angry, the temperatures had
dropped, and the wind had risen. By early afternoon parents were
hurrying to beat the storm and pick up their kids from school. But
Dad had taken Mom far away to the hospital; he couldn't come for
my little sister and me. So we had set out on foot, guided by the
fences along the road and the sled tracks through the snow.

By the time we reached the house of our closest neighbor a mile
from home, daylight was fading, and the blizzard had struck with full
force, narrowing visibility to near zero. I should have stayed put for
the night. But fearing that Dad might have returned home and been
worried about us, I left my sister at the neighbor's and headed across
the pasture alone, confident that I could simply follow the sled
tracks right to our door.

The tracks were clear at first and easy to follow. But soon I could
trace them only with great difficulty by bending down and looking

directly in front of my toes. Sometimes fresh drifting snow blotted the tracks out completely for yards at a time. On the far side of one drift, suddenly I found I had lost the trail. Fighting panic, I laid my plan as Dad had taught me. I would keep the wind on my back, and in a few minutes I would surely run into some part of the pasture fence. Then, I could simply follow the fence around to the gate and get back on track. But the wind kept shifting, and I wandered through darkness and howling wind for what seemed like hours.

Finally, near exhaustion, I came upon a fence, then found a gate, spotted the trail, saw the lights from a house…. But rather than being at home, I was back where I had started, at our neighbor's!

Where had I gone wrong? I had been so confident. How and where had I lost my trail?

Diane lost her way and her confidence as well. She, too, wondered when and how she had gotten off track. "I just don't understand it," she mused. "Three years ago, my faith was the most important thing in my life. Now I am just as active in church, but usually I would rather be someplace else. At home, I keep finding excuses to skip my quiet times, and prayer just feels like I'm talking to myself.

"I've dropped hints about my doubts to several of my Christian friends—just to see if they feel the same way. But nothing I say seems to connect; obviously, they don't have the same problem.

"So," Diane asked me, "what went wrong? Where did all these doubts come from?"

How do any of us—especially those of us who really have wanted God—come to the point that we are bothered with doubts? What factors in our lives lead us to question God's presence, or His love, or His relevance, or His *very existence?* And what circumstances influence the particular shape of our doubts?

We human beings are complex and mysterious creatures. So we'll likely never completely uncover all the answers to those questions. And that may not really be necessary. You don't need to retrace your whole journey just to get moving again on the road of faith. And yet some understanding of the factors contributing to your particular experience of doubt can be very helpful in getting your faith back on track. Here's why:

First, what you are experiencing might not be doubt at all. There's always the chance that your problem is emotional or physical or even environmental rather than spiritual—or that factors in your past are causing you to hang the doubt label where it doesn't belong.

Second, even if your doubt is real, certain baggage from your past journey may be weighing you down in your progress toward faith.

An elementary understanding of the factors that are shaping your doubt can help you handle your doubt more wisely.

Third, choosing the way to deal with your doubt may depend on where your doubt came from. Sometimes it's better to wrestle actively with your questions, and other times it makes more sense to lie low for a while and pay attention to other areas of your life. You may be sorely in need of spiritual support and refreshment, or you may need more exercise, regular meals, or even a session or two with a counselor. Even an elementary understanding of the factors that are shaping your doubt can help you handle your doubt more wisely.

With this in mind, let's look briefly at some of the circumstances that can shape your doubt.

DOUBT AND YOUR TEMPERAMENT

Some people, to begin with, seem to have doubt built into their very beings. I am one of these—what I call a "congenital doubter."

You wonder what a congenital doubter is? Then you probably are not one (although you may know several). We are the twelve-year-olds who kick rocks down the road, wondering if there really is a God, suspicious that there may be no one listening to our prayers, wondering why God never talks to us, and what if…what if…what if. We are the adults who are haunted by "existential angst"—a fundamental sense of uncertainty about the basics of existence—and tend to be plagued with troubling questions that we can't sweep under the rug.

We don't mean to be obnoxious, and we do not want to be rebellious or irreverent. Many of us, in fact, long to be doubt-free. We envy those who seem to be congenital believers, for whom faith just seems to come naturally. We even envy those of you who feel *out of touch* with God, feel *ignored* by God, or even feel *rebellion* toward God—because at least you do not seem to doubt *the existence* of God, you just doubt His interest in you or your ability to connect with Him.

We congenital doubters, on the other hand, often have trouble believing He is even there at all. And these doubts are rooted deep in our personality. Experts may disagree on where these doubts come from, but it *feels* like we were born with them!

But as we have seen, doubt can strike from a variety of angles, and it strikes those who are not natural doubters just as painfully as it strikes us doubting types. I suspect, in fact, that the reasons faith goes flat are as numerous as the human beings who experience doubt.

It is possible, for example, that doubt (or faith, for that matter) feels and looks different to one disposition or personality type than it does to another.

We hear a lot in pop psychology these days about temperaments, or inborn personality types. (These are actually based on the "four humors" described by the Greek physician Galen, who lived around 200 B.C.) People with differing temperaments perceive reality differently. Perhaps they doubt reality differently as well.

> It is possible that doubt feels and looks different to one disposition or personality type than it does to another.

One temperament is commonly called *sanguine*, meaning, literally, "from the blood." Perhaps this is you: passionate, eagerly optimistic, outgoing, and cheerful. A person with this temperament may believe easily at an emotional level. But when faith demands trudging through the blahs—when the presence of God cannot be experienced emotionally—the sanguine personality may quickly become vulnerable to doubt.

Galen called the calm, sluggish, peace-loving, and relatively unemotional temperament *phlegmatic*. People with this temperament may desire and expect very little color, drama, or emotion with their faith. Rather, "St. Phlegmatic" may latch on to promises such as "Being justified by faith, we have peace." But when the waters get rough or life becomes chaotic, he or she becomes uneasy and may begin to ask, "Where is God?"

The third temperament is called *choleric*; it applies to the hard-driving, "get things done" kind of person. Possibly faith comes easiest for cholerics when God does things the choleric's way. But when God changes the choleric's plans or inconveniences him or her, the choleric easily doubts the goodness, and maybe even the existence of God.

The fourth temperament is the *melancholic*. Melancholics tend to be analytical, exacting, contemplative, artistic, and moody. This disposition may be that of the classic rock kicker. Melancholics tend to approach faith abstractly, reflectively. They long for the kind of faith that fills a philosophical void and calms restless anxiety. This temperament continually explores the underside of faith, looking for intellectual cohesiveness and hidden meanings. Melancholics tend to scorn unexamined faith; they are the types who are always asking why.

People with a melancholic temperament may also find difficulty separating chronic *depression* from chronic doubt. And this brings us to yet another influence that can shape our doubts.

DOUBT AND YOUR UPS AND DOWNS

Faith does not necessarily wear an effervescent smile. In fact, "the real thing" sometimes comes in sackcloth and ashes, covered with scars, bathed with tears. One does not need to be up all the time in order to have faith. But—and here's the rub—some of us have trouble believing that.

I tend to be an emotional pushover; to pretend otherwise would be as phony as a campaign promise. Consequently, I am easily confused by mood swings, and I still have a lot to learn about separating my physical/emotional ups and downs from the realities of spiritual well-being.

Occasionally I pass through long, arid periods of semi-depression, longing to experience some "real religion." I moan with David the psalmist, "How long, O Lord, how long?" but usually keep plodding on across these wastelands, wondering if I will ever again feel anything deeply enough to weep over or to shout about.

I have often associated these low emotional cycles in one-to-one ratio with lack of faith. In actual fact, however, they often result from something very simple—fatigue, low blood sugar, a blown assignment, a nagging critic…or a prostate infection!

Then, when I break through to a season of physical vitality, emotional vibrancy, and positive thinking, I tend to assume this is when faith is strongest and that I am most certainly running on the spiritual fast track. The only blemish on these glorious times is the fear of losing them.

As a result of equating emotional upswings with faith, I often find myself clinging to the highs, dreading the lows, and contriving pump-up techniques to get me back up again. Actually these highs may not be "seasons of refreshing from the Lord's presence" at all, but may result merely from such simple things as a few good nights' rest, some regular exercise, a project that worked, a couple of affirming letters…and some antibiotic for the prostate!

So the long look has helped me put my mood swings in perspective and to identify them for what they usually are—mood swings. They come and go, sometimes with predictable rhythm and at other times with surprising suddenness; they are quite normal and usually temporary. They really have very little to do with the vibrancy of my faith! So sometimes the way to deal with the doubts is simply to wait, pray, and plug away—or spend a couple of days at the lake!

Though my emotions may flap like a flag in a gale, I am learning to trust that God doesn't move. He is the same, yesterday, today, and forever. He promised, "I will never leave you or forsake you." He is often doing the biggest work in us when we feel the lowest. The mountain peaks are fun, but the thin soil on the summit is not nearly so nourishing of spiritual fruit as that rich, dark humus in the valleys.

If I learn to distinguish my mood swings from my doubts, I can concentrate on learning the lessons God has to teach me. It's not easy to make this distinction, but remembering that I don't always have to be up to have faith can be a big help.

DOUBT AND THE SEASONS OF YOUR LIFE

Mood swings aren't the only ups and downs most people experience in the course of their lives. We go through normal life cycles or life seasons over the longer term as well, and these predictable change points produce fluctuations that can profoundly affect our faith/doubt feelings.

Perhaps the most obvious of these changes occurs in adolescence, when profound physical changes and major developmental challenges may spur us to question everything we have ever believed. But adolescence is far from the last life change that may affect our faith.

In a circus tent, spectators watch the big rings in the center, not the entrances and exits. Yet until recent years, in the study of life, we have looked more at child development and old age than we have at the main events in the middle of adult life.[1] A well-worn proverb has summarized the prevailing attitude: "Children change, but adults just age."

Nowadays, however, we realize that adults go through predictable stages of development just as children and adolescents do. These stages of development can impact our doubt/faith cycles as well. Faith may feel different, and doubt may change faces with the changing seasons of life.

In my observation, the experience of adult life cycles can be likened to a lobster's shedding its shell. Lobsters repeatedly go through the trauma of losing the old shell, being vulnerable and sensitive for a while, then toughening and forming a new shell. We, too, undergo successive periods of vulnerability, and each of these leaves us open to doubt.

In early adulthood, for example, many of us lose our inno-cence. We begin a life's work, maybe marry, set goals for our career. And then we tend to feel confused because we discover that just doing a good job does not guarantee success…and that marriage is not always bliss…and that there may be more than one right way to approach a problem. As we lose our illusions and our innocence, it stands to reason that we may start wondering if faith, too, is an illusion—or at least radically different from what we thought it was supposed to be.

Gradually, however, our shell starts to grow. Most of us settle down and establish homes, build intimate relationships and net-works of acquaintances. We put down roots, position ourselves, and concentrate on climbing the mountain of success.

At that point, usually in our midthirties, many of us reach another period of vulnerability. Not the upheaval of adolescence. Not the big questions of the twenties, nor the storms of midlife—we just get bogged down in the complexity of our lives. We get higher up the mountain, only to discover there is another mountain and another. We alter our dreams and make compromises. Stress begins to erode the intimacy of our relationships.

During these years, faith is often simply shoved to the margins of life. Or it sometimes—in the form of institutional religious activity—becomes part of the clutter and pressure. Involvement in religious organizations substitutes for a personal relationship with God; the result is less trust and more stress. No wonder many believers have doubts during their thirties!

During midlife we usually lose another shell. Often triggered by trouble—a business failure, a marriage problem, worries about chil-dren, a dead-end career, or a health problem—midlife turbulence sometimes even escalates to the crisis point. And like a second adolescence, midlife can bring body change, mood swings, social insecurity, and identity questions.

Men and women in midlife often feel surrounded by enemies. Jobs become more complex when interest in them may be declin-ing. Family costs more and seems to be around less. Self-pity lurks near, and it's easy to blame God for what is happening. Biblical faith can come up for grabs or even be dropped, yet most believers eventually recover and move on through this white water into the gentler streams of later midlife.

A decade or so later, life often pushes us to ask, "Is there nothing more?" We face three big *D*s: decline, depression, and death. When time is running out, faith may face its biggest test as the supreme organizing and stabilizing reality. Some people at this stage confess a fear that they have believed all these years for nothing. Yet others find their faith is stronger than ever, although less experiential and less cause-oriented. Faith in the late years is often quieter, deeper, and more matter-of-fact than in earlier decades.

> When time is running out, faith may face its biggest test as the supreme organizing and stabilizing reality.

DOUBT AND YOUR PAINFUL PAST

Not all doubts are related to normal ups and downs and generational life cycles, of course. Many are more personal, stemming from individual experience. The unique events that shape our individual lives uniquely shape our individual faith and doubts as well.

Some doubts can be traced to painful chapters in the struggler's emotional history. Mary, for example, who was passed through a dozen foster homes after being abandoned by her parents, doesn't think she can trust anyone—even God.

And then there was Sheldon, who adored his youth minister and his parents until his mom had an affair with the youth minister and left Sheldon's dad. Sheldon says, "My flimsy feelings of faith don't stand a chance against the anger I feel toward anything that smells like religion."

Rachel was emotionally abused and humiliated for years by her whole family. Now her self-esteem crawls on its belly. She feels she will never be worthy of God, so "What's the use?" She tries to seal God out of her reality.

Susan grew up in an intensely religious family that constantly bickered and complained. Every Sunday after church she dined on broiled preacher, fricasseed youth minister, fried worship leader, and bitterly roasted elders. By the time Susan turned eighteen, faith had left a terrible taste in her mouth. "If that is what God does to people, who needs it?"

Possibly the most common faith impediment cropping up out of doubters' emotional histories is related to parental abuse. That is why when many bow their heads to pray, they choke on the phrase "Our Father." Life has loaded that word with a cargo of negative emotional baggage.

Daisy's father was both abusive and distant. Her mother was caring and tender-natured, but adhered compulsively to a rigidly authoritarian view of religion. Small wonder Daisy sometimes has a difficult time sorting out God, mother, and father from one another.

"When I don't want to believe," she says, "unbelief feels like freedom from God's rules. I have too many rules of my own." But Daisy blinks back tears as she reflects. "When I want to believe, it is because things might be easier. Less hassle with my religious husband. Maybe I would be more at peace. And it would be great to feel that there is someone out there big and powerful enough to take care of me; someone who is positive, and cares, like a mother."

Then Daisy's voice takes on a cold edge as she declares, "If there is a God, God is a mother. Mothers care about you. The God in the Bible is cruel, like a dad. An egomaniac who wants us to worship Him and bow and scrape at His every beck and call. I don't like God. I can't see Him wanting good for anybody."

At least one psychologist contends that unbelief may actually result from psychological scars—especially painful father experiences. New York University psychology professor Paul Vitz, in his book *Faith of the Fatherless*, studied the childhoods of several well-known atheists and saw strong evidence that their rejection of God is directly related to father pain: the death of a father or abuse or abandonment by their fathers.

Vitz points out that Friedrich Nietzsche, the philosopher who declared that "God is dead," lost his father at age four. Samuel

Butler, skeptical British writer, was often brutally beaten by his "pious" father. Sigmund Freud said his father was a "pervert" and built much of his psychological theory around father hatred. John Paul Sartre, French existentialist, lost his father when he was a baby and later deeply resented his stepfather. Joseph Stalin's father beat him unmercifully, so Vitz suggests that it should not surprise us that a communism which rejected authority figures, including God, appealed to Stalin. Adolf Hitler received terrible beatings from his father. And the father of China's communist leader, Mao Zedong, was a tyrant. Madalyn Murray O'Hair once tried to kill her father with a butcher knife. Many more names are included in Vitz's list of pain-shaped unbelief. Vitz suggests that after studying these and other "major historical rejecters of God…we find a weak, dead or abusive father in every case." Consequently Vitz urges great compassion for atheists, because behind their unbelief, in all likelihood lies some painful memory.

So as you examine your doubts, you may want to honestly confront the possibility that one of your roadblocks to faith may be some pain from your past.

DOUBT AND YOUR TIMES OF CRISES

Yes, scars from deep in the secret caverns of our emotional history, coming in all shapes and sizes, can arrive at the surface disguised as doubt. But pressure points and crisis events can also shape doubts more directly, even for people with healthy emotional histories. It's not uncommon for a crisis or a series of crises—a job loss, illness, bereavement—to push us to doubt or escalate niggling doubts to dangerous levels. (That's precisely why bad experiences are often called "tests of faith.")

Dean may have spoken for a lot of us. Nearly fifty people piled into Nathan and Tammy's living room to pray. And pray we did, fervently and out loud. Inwardly, however, some of us were smothering in a cloud of doubt. Would God answer our prayers and spare Shannon?

Shannon was five years old. When she was four, a softball-sized malignancy was removed from her little body, taking one kidney with it. During the next few months, she received heavy chemotherapy and did great for a long while. Sunday morning faces beamed as Shannon and her friends proudly bounced down the aisles at our church to gather the visitors' cards at the close of the service.

But later that week Shannon's parents, Gerald and Alice, got the bad news. The malignancy had invaded Shannon's lungs and was spreading fast. Several other danger signals made the prognosis less than encouraging. Specialists recommended desperate measures—experimental radiation and chemotherapy.

Alice and Gerald took Shannon out of the hospital to spend a weekend at the lake before the treatments were to begin. Shannon's grandfather and her uncle and aunt gathered with the rest of us for prayer.

Along with the prayer, tears and embraces were shared. After one long silence, Dean, Shannon's uncle, began to pray, "Dear God, why are you doing this to us? We are a good family; we've been Christians. Shannon is the only grandchild in the family, and she has brought us so much joy. We need her to bring us life. God, I don't know how much you need her, but we need her more than you!"

All of us were wondering—as so many others have wondered in similar circumstances—why God would allow such things as cancer in innocent children. On what basis would He grant some people the gift of healing but not others? Our hearts were breaking for Gerald and Alice, wondering how they—and we—would feel about God if, after we had prayed so fervently for something that seemed so obviously right, He would not grant our request to spare Shannon's life.

The sad story on Shannon ended in her premature death. But Dean's questions—and our questions—are still alive and often plague us in the form of doubts when we are confronted with unexplainable difficulty.

Where is God...when such a thing can happen to us or the people we love?

Possibly this kind of pain lay behind the well-known doubt of the disciple Thomas, who refused to believe in Jesus' resurrection until he saw the risen Lord with his own eyes.[2] It is possible that Thomas may have had congenital doubter tendencies—or at least an undercurrent of niggling doubt—all along. But his doubts appear to he driven to the surface by the stunning shock and ensuing stress of Jesus' arrest, trial, and execution.

Talk about a major life crisis! Thomas's hopes, his dreams, and his confidence that he was on the inside track to truth all crashed and burned in just a few hours! No wonder Thomas seems to have temporarily lost his faith. No wonder he wanted proof!

And life crises can easily produce "doubting Thomases" in our day as well. Maybe you can relate.

DOUBT AND THE PACE OF OUR LIVES

But it's not just the ups and down of our personal lives that feed our doubts. I suspect that the fast pace of contemporary culture also takes its toll on our faith.

Since the days of Thomas and of Ketar, there have always been some believers who were plagued with doubts. Even in centuries when times were quiet and simple, many believers had difficulty "hearing God." During my own young manhood, even though in more modern times, I, too, moved through a simple, quiet world at a leisurely pace. Yet I wrestled with doubt and seemed to hear no word from heaven.

In our day, however, the doubt-plot thickens. That is, the speed, secularism, and sound levels of today's world assault our senses like a blizzard wind and complicate the problem of dealing with doubt. In our fast-paced, high-decibel culture, God's "still, small voice" can be difficult to discern, and it's easy to wonder whether He's saying anything at all.

One significant doubt breeder is *cognitive overload*. The media bring too much of the whole world at once to every living room. We are wearied by what we see and hear and smell around us. Many days we feel not so much like banks from which people have made withdrawals but rather like garbage cans into which everybody has dumped something.

We are sick to death of parents who beat the life out of their children, criminals who rape and murder, military buildups, school violence, and white-collar hoods who drive BMWs. We are weary of religious events and church bureaucracy. We are tired of inhaling smog, listening to jackhammers, and seeing the gaudy banners that festoon the gas station next to a franchised twenty-four-hour convenience store, next to a franchised chicken stand, next to a...

One significant doubt breeder is cognitive overload.

Under the cumulative impact of the stuff we expose ourselves to, no wonder we're emotionally black and blue—and cynical. We are taking a bludgeoning.

In this kind of world, faith is no luxury; it's a necessity! But in this kind of world, faith can also be hard to come by.

Overstimulation, too, fights against faith in our modern culture. And we want it that way. We insist that some form of media fills every second of our downtime. We expect the headlines to scream at us even if there is nothing to scream about. We eagerly slap down our cash for movies that begin with the destruction of the world and then escalate to a more exciting climax. Bombarded with such internal and external racket, how will we ever hear a still, small voice? Not much of value gets through to us, and what does really doesn't go in very deep.

We are also bogged down with *overcommitment*. We are so busy running to answer a thousand calls—work, family, church, sporting events, social issues, civic demands—that we find no time for reflecting and listening; besides, we are too exhausted. Activism, no matter how well-intentioned, leaves life shallow. It can also leave us with faith that may appear to be a mile wide but may not be an inch deep.

Finally, we live in a highly *secularized* society—one dominated by materialistic and utilitarian assumptions. Although surveys tell us that God remains important to approximately 95 percent of North

Americans,[3] the nerve-centers of powerful influence such as the media, the educational establishment, and the political infrastructure often treat questions of faith as outmoded, beneath the dignity of enlightened people, or downright irrelevant. And whether you see this trend as a dangerous slide toward immorality or a healthy separation of church and state, one bottom-line result is that faith has lost the sanction of society. Instead, skepticism is the dominant mode of thought—and doubt flourishes in such an atmosphere.

DOUBT AND THE UNSEEN WORLD

All the factors we have seen—temperament, mood swings, life cycles, past history, present crisis, and cultural environment—can pull at our faith. All deserve consideration as we examine the shape of our doubt.

But there's another consideration, of course. Doubt has real spiritual implications.

HARM FROM BELOW?

The Bible indicates that doubt can be a sign of spiritual danger. We are surrounded by spiritual forces that are hostile to faith. In fact, doubt can be a tool of the Father of Lies—a temptation that threatens to separate us from our desperately needed fellowship with God.

Put that way, some doubt is closely connected with human temptation and sin. But that shouldn't be a surprise. Scripture says that we human beings, left to our own devices, are by definition sinful and spiritually blind. After all, that's the whole point in Christ's coming. That's why we need "help with our unbelief."

What am I saying? Simply that exploring the psychological, emotional, and even physical factors that shape your doubt does not rule out doubt's *spiritual* significance. Yes, feelings of doubt are shaped by our individual makeup and our personal histories, but doubt is not just a psychic hiccup—any more than God himself is a projection of our needy psyches.

Doubt, in other words, is serious. It's worth grappling with, even over a long period, because the stakes are high. But grappling with doubt isn't entirely up to us either. If we want to believe, we *will* find help for our unbelief.

In fact, other spiritual forces—besides the Prince of Darkness—may be at work in our doubt feelings as well!

HELP FROM ABOVE

Some people think themselves doubters during times when the heavens are silent, and they really wonder if God is there. He seems to be out of touch. Henri Nouwen refers to this experience as "the absence of God." Possibly all believers occasionally feel this way.

However, some of these times when God seems absent may actually be the work of His grace. By "withdrawing from us a sense of His presence," He may actually be refining our faith for the long run. As Nouwen says, "His absence…is often so deeply felt that it leads to a new sense of His presence. This is powerfully expressed in Psalm 22:1: 'My God, my God, why have you forsaken me?'"[4]

To illustrate: Although I love my wife, Carolyn, enormously, quite often I take her for granted when we are together. I rarely find myself reflecting specifically on her unique traits and qualities. But when I am separated from her for days in a row, I miss her painfully, and I find myself focusing on particulars I seem unaware of when we are together. Memory and longing call to mind and vividly contemplate all sorts of details about her: the ways she walks or stands, the color of her eyes, the way her hands hold flowers, the sound of her laugh, the touch of her skin, how she smells or feels, how she thinks.

In a sense, Carolyn is sometimes more completely in my consciousness in her absence than in her presence.

Possibly when we feel that God is absent, He, too, may be more completely and sharply focused in our conscious thoughts, more so than when we take for granted that He is very near. Again, to quote Nouwen:

> The mystery of God's presence, therefore, can be touched only by a deep awareness of his absence. It is in the center of our longing for the absent God that we discover his footprints…. In

the patient waiting for the loved one, we discover how much he has filled our lives already. Just as the love of a mother for her son can grow deeper when he is far away, just as children can learn to appreciate their parents more when they have left the home, just as lovers can rediscover each other during long periods of absence, so our intimate relationship with God can become deeper and more mature by the purifying experience of his absence.[5]

Perhaps then, rather than being cycles of doubt, these periods of God's "absence" may actually be visitations of grace during which we more specifically contemplate Him and He paradoxically becomes more completely "present."

THE COLOR OF YOUR DOUBT

So how about you? Can you recognize fragments of yourself in any of the stories I have told here? Is it possible that your unique brand of doubt is related to your basic temperament or to your particular stage in life or to a negative experience either long past or recent? Can you see the possibility of God's grace at work in your questions?

Chances are, of course, that all these factors—temperament, history, spiritual temptation, and God's grace—shape your doubt to a certain extent. And chances are that you'll never entirely sort out where your doubt came from.

So what can you do? How can faith in God be renewed and flourish as you travel through the doubt-producing circumstances of life?

Keep on reading; we're getting there.

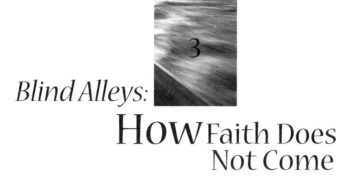

Blind Alleys: HOW Faith Does Not Come

A classic painting depicts Jesus knocking on a door with no knob on it. Obviously, the artist means we can only open the heart from the inside. But my friend Jack says he has always wanted to paint the picture from the other side of the same door, with a human hand groping in the dark for the knob but not being able to find it.

Letting God in is not always easy. Some of us are honestly trying to get closer to God—to let Him into our hearts—but we keep getting blocked. And it's not just because we have trouble hearing His knock. Even when we hear, sometimes we can't seem to find the doorknob!

For centuries doubters have been attempting to reach faith through a number of popular avenues that seem appealing but actually turn out to be blind alleys.

One long-ago monk, for instance, whose story I encountered while poking through a library at Escoreal, Spain, felt the need to bolster his teetering faith, so he copied the entire Bible out by hand. All, that is, except James through Revelation. Somewhere in the late chapters of Hebrews, still tormented by doubts, the young Spanish cleric shot himself.

And today people are still trying to get belief by traveling roads that do not lead to faith, ways by which faith does *not* come. And that includes some of the standard "Christian" routes recommended by earnest but inexperienced or ill-informed spiritual guides.

You likely know some people who never miss a service, but whose faith, despite their churchgoing, seems warped. They may be bitter, for instance, or selfish or petty. And they are living proof that sitting in a church will no more make a mature believer out of you than sitting in a garage will make you an automobile.

Joyce joined five Bible study groups to erase her doubts and build her faith. She was seen last Saturday leaving Cisero's Disco at four in the morning and wondering in slurred speech to her escort how she came to hate all fifty of those Bible-thumping women at once.

Stewart just finished his Ph.D. in New Testament Greek. He enrolled in seminary hoping that the religious environment could get him past his nagging doubts. But although he went in hungry for God, he left gorged on Greek. Today, Stewart is trying to find a publisher for his first book, *Why I Am an Agnostic*.

Charles is spending more time at church than ever before but enjoying it less. He feels guilty because he cannot do more. He desperately seeks to have a cheery-faced and clear-eyed faith like Fred's, and he has been told that if he keeps at it and involves himself in more Christian service, he will eventually find it. Actually Charles feels farther and farther from God. He hasn't prayed alone in months.

Have you met any of these people? They are doubters who want stronger faith. But they are wasting their time, because they are going about it in all the wrong ways. And they are not alone.

This chapter will erect warning signs at the entrance to some blind alleys that can lure us off the pathway to faith.

Later we will examine some ways faith *does* come. Right now, here are some commonly attempted approaches through which faith *does not* come!

BLIND ALLEY #1: TURNING OFF YOUR MIND

First, *faith does not come by squinching up our eyes and trying with all our might to believe what we know isn't so.*

In the opening chapter of *A Reasonable Faith,* Tony Campolo relates an enlightening encounter that took place when he was on the teaching faculty of a large Ivy League university. A graduate student had come to him for help in dealing with severe guilt and sorrow over the loss of her fiance. Despite Campolo's efforts to comfort, to explain, and finally to argue her back into a state of revived faith in God, he knew he had failed. "I want to believe you. Don't you understand that?" she exclaimed. "But I can't make myself believe it."[1]

True, faith does begin with a desire to believe—but wanting to believe does not mean ignoring all the obstacles to belief. The will to believe is not the same thing as self-deception or wishful thinking or brainwashing. Ignoring troublesome doubts and sweeping them under the rug will not make them go away. They must be faced honestly!

> Ignoring the questions did not make them go away; it just eroded my confidence in the honesty (or the intelligence) of believers.

During some of my painful periods of doubt, I reasoned, "Since so many of these believers I meet are obviously much better informed than I, they surely will have thought of all the formidable questions and problems that hinder my faith. And yet they believe. I wonder how? Maybe they just ignore the issues that bother them."

I made a stab at doing exactly that, but my own questions just wouldn't stay under the rug. The only way I could keep them there was to fool myself or to be intellectually dishonest. And I couldn't believe God requires either as part of the price of believing in Him who said, "I am the...truth."[2]

Besides, ignoring the questions did not make them go away; it just eroded my confidence in the honesty (or the intelligence) of believers. Of course, this made faith seem even more ethically and psychologically unhealthy to me.

In fact, trying to believe by ignoring one's doubts only brings about the disintegration of one's own integrity, leading farther into confusion. No! Faith does not come simply by closing your eyes to anything that challenges your belief.

BLIND ALLEY #2: WAITING FOR FAITH TO HAPPEN

Second, *faith does not come by merely waiting till faith "happens"*— although faith *does* usually develop over time. Back during those days of kicking rocks down country roads, I finally settled for the hope that one day, somehow, faith would happen to me as I got older. After all, I was only a kid at the time. "Maybe when I reach high school," I hope-wished, "then I will believe."

But my friend Doubt still roomed with me when I went away to high school. My childhood questions grew into a suspicion that I might never be able to keep the standards or to trust the One who set them. Rather than giving peace and purpose, God seemed only to intensify my guilt and feelings of hopelessness. I would repeatedly approach faith, only to recoil from the pain it seemed to bring. Sometimes I felt that the closer I drew to God, the more He hurt me! Still, I continued to hope that one day—perhaps in college—I would "grow into" a comfortable faith.

But then in college I was confronted by even more formidable faith challenges. Ironically I enrolled to study for the ministry— perhaps in the hope that the studies would teach me how to believe. But even my theological studies did not drive away the dogged doubts that continued to nip at my heels. Instead, I was exposed to intellectual problems I had previously not even imagined: What in Scripture is myth and what is history? Are New Testament writers really honest in their use of the Old Testament? Why do millions in foreign lands, virtually untouched by Christianity, appear to be served quite well by their religions? Why do bad things happen to good people—and good things to bad?

I read things from science, psychology, and philosophy that

didn't seem to square with the Bible, and those contradictions certainly didn't clear away my doubts. No, faith didn't come by waiting till college.

The years of adulthood since have only further dismantled my illusion that merely waiting might bring faith. On the contrary, simply waiting for faith actually seemed to lead farther into doubt.

Blind Alley #3: Getting an Offer You Can't Refuse

Third, although faith *is* a divine gift, *it does not come by arbitrary divine fiat,* as if some people were destined for faith and some for unbelief, with nothing either group can do about it.

Yes, from God's perspective, faith is a gift. The Bible says so clearly.[3] But God does not force anyone to accept His gift. From our perspective, faith begins when a person chooses to trust God's gift.[4]

To state it in theological jargon, the sovereign Spirit prompts us to choose faith, but He also allows us the power to refuse His promptings. *Faith is a decision of the heart and will to entrust ourselves to God.*

Sound complicated? A friend tells a story that may help explain the paradoxical relationship between "gift" and "choice."

This friend was offered an unusual gift from someone: a weekend in Las Vegas, including tickets and table reservations at a top Vegas show. He was told simply to give this man's name to the maître d'.

At the door, my friend joined a long line of impatient people who were dressed to the nines. (He wore jeans, a sport coat, and an open-necked shirt.) Disgruntled people kept leaving the head of the line, and a big man in a black tux kept shouting, "Sorry. Sold out." Some were offering the maître d' as much as two hundred dollars above the ticket price to get in. My friend only had twenty or so dollars in his jeans pocket. What should he do?

He stayed in line till he stood in front of the maître d', who gave him a blank stare and repeated, "Sorry, sold out." He was about to leave but then remembered to mention his friend's name.

The big man in the black tux brightened, "Oh, sorry. Right this way."

As he explained later, "I had no status or money that could have earned my way in. I hadn't even bought a ticket. Plenty around me appeared to have far more going for them. But on the mention of this man's name, I had full access. That was gift-grace."

However, my friend also made a choice! The maître d' would not have forced him to go in. Entrance was a gift, but it still would not have been his without his choice to go to Las Vegas and claim it. He had the power to turn around and leave. Receiving the gift or rejecting it was his free choice.

Faith, too, is a gift of God for which we don't have the resources to muster and which we don't deserve. And *unlike* my friend's Las Vegas weekend, faith is a gift offered to all of us, equally, by God. Jesus said, "Come to me, *all* you who are weary and burdened."[5] Each of us, however, must make the decision whether or not to accept God's free gift. Faith is an offer we can refuse.

BLIND ALLEY #4: LOOKING FOR DEFINITIVE PROOF

Fourth, *faith does not come through logical* proof—although faith *is* supported by ample evidence and is far from an irrational leap in the dark. We cannot be logically forced to believe.

I used to go fishing with a friend who apparently hoped to get his faith through logical proof. "Just convince me," he would challenge. "I'll argue against God's existence. You argue for it. Give me your best shot, and if you win the argument, you'll have a believer. I am no fool. When I see the clear proof, I will have to believe!"

The outstanding Texas historian J. Frank Dobie had my fishing buddy's number. With tongue planted firmly in cheek, he told a "conversion story" that wryly hints at the shortcomings of the prove-it approach to faith:

They fit for forty minutes
And the crowd would whoop and cheer

When Jack spit up a tooth or two,
Or when Bobby lost an ear.
But at last Jack got him under
And lie slugged him oncet or twicet,
And straightway Bob admitted
The divinity of Christ....
Then someone brought a bottle out
And kindly passed it round....
...And the spread of infidelity
Was checked in camp that day.[6]

That's an absurd story, of course. Faith does not come by having the truth beaten into us by someone who can slug harder than we can. And faith certainly does not come by being "argued into it" by a brighter, better informed, and more articulate person. The heart just doesn't work that way!

Think about it. If cold logic and hard facts forced people to believe in God, then the smarter people would be the first to believe, and the duller people would be the last. Sometimes it seems that the opposite may actually be true. Intelligence levels have little to do with faith.

On the one hand, you don't have to be a dummy to be "gullible enough to have faith." On the other hand, being an unbeliever obviously does not mean being stupid. There are plenty of intelligent unbelievers out there.

One reason faith doesn't come from proof is that conclusive proof in the form of rational argument is simply not available!

Robert recalls how his faith floundered when he attempted to arrive at faith by pitting arguments in support of faith against those counter to faith in God. "If my proof is solid," Robert reasoned to himself, "I will have no choice but a life-changing faith."

But Robert never could be sure he had heard the last word. "Beneath every rock I turned," he remembers, "I would discover three or four more rocks unturned. So my faith hung in limbo. I literally worried that I wasn't smart enough to hold on to my faith. At any given moment, a brighter mind than mine might torpedo my best arguments and blow my faith out of the waters."

Ultimately, everyone who decides either for or against faith must make that decision without all the facts.

The problem, of course, is that in an argument over faith, neither "side" can ever be sure it has heard all of the arguments.

I've heard it told that a long-ago president of Princeton University tried regularly to convert his good friend, the president of Harvard. Although the Harvard man thought he might be a believer someday, he deferred year after year, saying, "I must examine all the information first."

Finally his friend from Princeton said, "To complete every course listed in Harvard's catalog would take at least a hundred years. And that would only cover the courses currently offered in just one university. And there are thousands of universities. You cannot live long enough to examine all available information. Now just what information do you need to know before you can believe?"

Ultimately, everyone who decides either for or against faith must make that decision without all the facts. Besides, having all the solid information may not persuade us anyway. The heart looms ever larger than the head when it comes to deciding the direction of a life. The resistant heart can always find a quibble or a dodge, no matter how conclusive the "proof"!

Some believers are shocked to discover that the Bible never attempts proof for God. If faith comes this way, why did God not give us a book of proofs? Instead, from the first to the final lines, the Bible boldly *assumes* the reality of God!

The Psalms, for example, address God as one would a good friend. Who feels compelled to prove a friend exists? How strange that would seem!

Suppose I told you about my friend Lou Seckler, with whom I have traveled to several countries. After you heard several of my stories about Lou, what if you said to me, "Prove Lou Seckler exists." I would be stunned! Of course he exists! He is my friend!

But suppose I took up your challenge. I might say, "Well, some weeks I talk with him nearly every day. I have been at his house a number of times. I have a book he has written, several letters from him, and a painting he gave me. So, what more proof do you need?" That's the tack the Bible takes.

Obviously, that stance can be more than a little threatening, especially to us modern people who have been trained to demand proof for everything we believe. When a seminary professor pointed out in class that the Bible doesn't attempt to prove God, only assumes Him, a student countered, "This is kind of scary. Are you saying faith is a 'blind leap'?"

The professor answered, "Yes and no."

Yes—in one sense, if we have faith, at some point we will have made that decision to believe without complete proof and with a lot of questions unanswered.

On the other hand, no! Faith is not a *blind* leap. We are not suggesting that kind of faith Frederick Buechner describes as "the capacity to accept a lot of holy whoppers that an intelligent eighth grader would dismiss out of hand."[7] It's not the kind of faith indicted in Archie Bunker's loose interpretation of Mark Twain's definition: "Faith is believing what any fool knows ain't so."

Instead, faith is a leap based not on proof but on *trust*.

On August 23, 1864, Abraham Lincoln wrote out a memorandum on a piece of paper, folded it, and asked the entire cabinet of the United States to sign it without reading it.[8] Amazingly, they did! By so doing, they committed themselves to the consequence of Lincoln's proposals without having read them.

That's *strong* faith—but not *blind* faith! Lincoln's cabinet had plenty of reason to believe in their president's proposal, even though they had not actually read the document. They had no proof. They knew Lincoln well enough to trust him.

There is no life without trust, without faith. Every person believes in something. Daily existence depends on some kind of faith. We all have faith that the sun will rise tomorrow. Hasn't it done so for centuries? But no one can prove empirically that it will.

You trust the chair you sit on to support you, but you have no guarantee. It may have a sturdy track record, but what about the next time you sit on it?

We all believe the lights will come on when we flip the switch, the car will start when we turn the key, the elevator cable at the office will not break, the driver at the intersection will obey traffic signals.

But note three observations about these things we all believe in:

1. *We cannot prove any of them.* Granted, their track records make them believable. The lights have come on the last sixteen thousand times we flipped the switch. The elevator has worked for years. The drivers usually stop at traffic lights. But what about next time? You don't know about it. You believe it. You trust in it. You have faith in it.

2. *We understand very few of the things we trust every day.* Most of us could not explain electricity on a bet, but we still flip switches. The fact that something is incomprehensible to us does not destroy our faith in it.

3. *Our faith in all these things is based on evidence, not proof.* The cumulative evidence of past experience allows us to live our daily lives confidently trusting all these things that we cannot prove.[9]

There is a big difference between proof and evidence. Proof *establishes* conclusions. Evidence, while it may be quite persuasive, only *points toward* those conclusions. By trying to turn evidence into proof, we establish an impossible criterion for our faith and may actually be shoving God away from us.

But even though evidence is not the same as proof, examining the evidence for what we are asked to believe can pave the way to trust by clearing away some intellectual obstacles, so that our faith does not require us to park our brains at the church door. For me, the evidence undergirding the Christian faith is overwhelming and convincing. For this reason, in the appendix, I have listed some excellent books and tapes that offer faith-supporting evidence— often called apologetics. You may find them helpful as well.

Watch carefully, however. Since books and tapes are obviously written by human beings, they can easily be flawed, and some will even contain lethal distortions. During the 1950s, for example, college students devoured books by Harry Rimmer, a popular "Christian apologist." However, Rimmer's books actually harmed rather than helped many inquiring minds because Rimmer's "archaeology" and "history" were laced with fabrications. My appendix does not recommend "Rimmer quality" books. But keep the caution light glowing anyway; even the most serious books on apologetics may include some flaws. And even the most fair-minded and well-informed thinkers differ on their interpretation of the facts.

And this warning brings us back to the original point. Yes, apologetics has some value. But expecting apologetics to prove there is a God may backfire on us. For faith, by its very definition, is not *knowing*.

"We live by faith, not by sight" is the way the Bible puts it.[10] When something is verified by empirical data, it shifts out of the category called faith. Rather than being something we believe in, something we trust, it becomes something we know.

To go back to the example above, when I sit in my office chair, I do not accept its existence by faith. I know it is here by my five senses. (Yes, I can even smell and taste it!)

But we are dealing with God, who does not subject Himself to that kind of cross-examination. He has not presented Himself to the world in rational, empirical form. (If we could pin Him down like that, would He be God at all?) As one person said, "It is just as impossible to prove that God *does not* exist as to prove that He *does* exist!"

Besides, even if the existence of God could be proved "beyond reasonable doubt," proving God would not be likely to "scratch our itchy spot." As Frederick Buechner says,

We all want to be certain, we all want proof, but the kind of proof that we tend to want—scientifically or philosophically demonstrable proof that would silence all doubts once and for all—would not, in the long run, I think, answer the fearful depths of our need at all. For what we need to know, of course, is not just that God exists, not just that beyond the steely brightness of the stars there is a cosmic intelligence of some kind to keep the whole show going, but that there is a God right here in the thick of our day-by-day lives who may not be writing messages about himself in the stars but who in one way or another is trying to get messages through our blindness as we move around down here knee-deep in the fragrant muck and misery and marvel of the world. It is not objective proof of God's existence that we want but, whether we use religious language for it or not, the experience of God's presence. That is the miracle that we are really after. And that is also, I think, the miracle that we really get.[11]

I like that. Sure, we want solid foundations for our faith. But what most of us really want is *relationship with a personal God*. We want "peace with God."[12] We hunger "to know Christ."[13] We want a rich, close, intimate, meaningful, practical relationship with the Lord. And we don't develop a relationship through logical proof.

Faith is born when the Holy Spirit touches our hearts and then somewhere, at the center of our souls, awakens our wills and invites us to trust God. "If anyone *chooses* to do God's will," said Jesus, "he will *find out* whether my teaching comes from God."[14]

He woos, but we must still will.

He woos, but we must still will. We must make the faith decision. This is what believing is at its roots.

Apologetics clears the way for this faith decision. Evidence supports the decision. The Spirit prompts the heart. But the hour of decision happens in the will. Faith happens not when we are finally swayed by convincing arguments but when somewhere deep inside of us—and without conclusive proof—we take up the challenge Joshua put to the people of Israel many centuries ago: "Choose for yourselves this day whom you will serve."[15]

BLIND ALLEY #5: LOOKING FOR A MIRACLE

If faith does not come by proof, *neither does it come through miracles*. I am not suggesting there is nothing miraculous about faith or that faith does not believe in miracles. But witnessing miracles does not automatically generate faith.

George and his old golfing buddy Phillip often opened their hearts to each other while they walked the fairways. While I waited for them to play through, I couldn't help overhearing. George was a doubter who, like many of us at some time in life, pleaded, "If you are really there, God, show me a miracle that cannot be explained away, and I will have to believe in you."

"I don't know exactly what I was expecting," George confessed to Phillip, "but a miraculous manifestation would not likely have helped much. If a huge voice thundered out of nowhere, 'I love you,' I probably would have responded, 'What was that—thunder? Lord, if that was really you, write those words out in the sky.' And if God chose to spell out in huge letters, stretching from horizon to horizon, 'I LOVE YOU,' I probably would have squinted up at the sky, questioning, 'Hmmm. I see the smoke-writing, but I can't see the airplane!'"

Phillip responded, "Well, George, how big a miracle would it take? Would you demand that the Lord physically appear to you?"

"Probably," George ventured.

"If so, in what form?" Phillip countered.

"Maybe if He came in human form, I'd believe," George suggested.

"You would, huh?" Phillip said. "He actually did appear in human form to a whole crowd of people. Even worked a bunch of miraculous signs right in front of them! But some eyewitnesses simply attributed His miracles to the devil and then crucified him."

Phillip went on, "George, would you be convinced if you physically watched with your own eyes as Jesus brought back to life your friend who has been dead for three days?"

"I dunno. Maybe."

"It didn't convince some people in the Bible. After Jesus had raised Lazarus from the dead, like it says in John, chapter eleven, the religious big shots wanted to *kill Lazarus!* Yes! They were so stubborn that rather than trusting Jesus, they tried to destroy miraculous evidence!"

Although he was drifting out of earshot from me, Phillip's point came through loud and clear: Miraculous evidence in itself will not necessarily produce faith! Scripture agrees. The Gospel of John states that "even after Jesus had done all these miraculous signs in their presence," many people "still *would not* believe in him."[16]

What is even more disturbing: These people John was describing had resisted so long that John finally says, "For this reason they *could not* believe."[17]

What an ominous statement. Notice that the unbelief of the people John was describing was a *choice*. Faith in Jesus would have threatened their vested interests. Consciously or unconsciously, they had chosen to set their hearts against Christ and had continued choosing not to believe in spite of miraculous proof over a long period of time. Finally, their hearts so hardened that even the miraculous signs of Jesus himself would not touch them! It is possible to reject faith so often that we can wind up actually dismantling our believing machinery.

The mightiest signs and wonders cannot change our hearts! Only the Spirit of God can do that! Through the gospel, the Spirit of God can move us to choose faith. But even then, He will not force us—only touch us, convict us, call us on. How we respond is entirely up to us.

SO HOW DOES FAITH COME?

Faith, then, does not come through dishonesty or self-deception. Just waiting for it won't necessarily bring it about. Faith is a divine gift, but it is never forced upon us. And it doesn't happen through convincing proof or by witnessing miracles.

How, then, does faith come? What can *we* do about it? I'll suggest a practical plan of action in later chapters. But first, to make sure we don't stray too far from the trail, let's turn to the next chapter to sharpen the focus of our definition of faith.

PART 2

I Think I Believe,
but What
Exactly Is
Faith?

Those who believe they believe in God
but without passion in the heart,
without anguish of mind,
without uncertainty,
without doubt,
and even at times without despair,
believe only in the idea of God,
and not in God himself.
—MADELEINE L'ENGLE

What Faith Is Not

4

Years ago I quit playing racquetball with my daughter. She always walloped me, and then she would patronize me. One day I vented my frustration, thumping the heel of my racket on the wall and muttering something like, "What do I have to do to win this game?"

Michele explained condescendingly, "Ah, it's simple, Dad. Whenever it's your turn, just hit the ball back in bounds."

Of course her answer was no help. I already *knew* that. I just couldn't do it!

Maybe you feel this frustrated about your faith.

You know what to do; you just can't seem to do it! And that raises a thorny question: Do you sometimes think that God is a bit unfair?

After all, the Bible states flatly, "Without faith it is impossible to please God."[1] Jesus warned, "If you do not believe that I am the one I claim to be, you will indeed die in your sins."[2] And Paul the apostle actually asserts that unbelief is inexcusable![3] The Bible makes no bones about it: Faith is the key to relationship with God. Yet—and here is the rub—some of us seem unable to muster much faith at all.

Does God demand the impossible? Just believe. Just keep hitting the ball back in bounds. Indeed! "I understand what I need to do," you may lament, "but I just can't do it. Or could I be barking up the wrong tree because I do not understand what faith really is?"

That last question hits the bull's-eye. Some people define faith in ways that make believing impossible for them. In fact, garbled definitions of faith often block the road to real believing for most honest seekers.

This means that if we want to increase our faith, we had best make sure we know what faith is. And to get a clear shot at what faith is, we may first need to push aside some things that faith is *not*.

ROADBLOCK #1: HOOKED ON A FEELING

First of all, you may already have faith and not know it because you are chasing an illusory "experience." Firestorms of emotion are often mistaken for genuine encounters with God. But *faith is not a feeling*.

So many North Americans seem to want a buzz out of life: "Just do it!" "Grab all the gusto you can." Some take shortcuts to feeling good through aesthetic experiences, sports, and even work—or more destructively through overeating or substance abuse or no-holds-barred sex. So we should not be surprised to discover some forms of pop religion that equate religious feelings with faith in God.

We long for that "faith experience"—a special song to stir the heart or a devotional explosion that will bring us to spiritual ecstasy. We devour books, tapes, sermons, retreats, conferences, churches, even relationships, always longing for the "something" that will plug us in and turn us on. And when that happens, we assume, we will then have found that elusive experience called *faith*.

Sometimes we actually do get off on a burst of religious euphoria and hit a new high—only to fall into disillusionment when the high wears off. Roger did this—often. He especially remembers a time when, toward the finale of a rollicking good conference, he was gripped by new and powerful feelings that seemed surely to be that long-sought-for faith experience.

"Ah! This is it," he celebrated. "Praise God! I'll never be that dull-hearted plodder again." But by the time he rolled up in the driveway on Sunday afternoon, "the whole thing had worn off and I found myself back home, the same old plodding doubter who had left on Friday."

"The net result," Roger told me later, "was that I felt even more hopeless than before I went to the conference. I spent the next week wondering, 'If that wasn't it, will I ever get it?'"

Even if we do "get it," we run the risk of developing what Christian psychologists Stephen Arterburn and Jack Felton call "religious addiction." In their book *Toxic Faith*, Arterburn and Felton describe how getting hooked on religious feeling can undermine healthy faith:

> A low-key faith is not necessarily a second-class faith.

> Religious addicts don't worship God. They use spiritual lights to satiate the need to experience something other than the boredom and pain of their existence. They use activity to distract themselves from their tough reality. They pervert what God intended for good. Seeking faith in God, they become so diverted by the experience and activity that they miss God.... The intended focus of real faith is distorted and perverted, lost in the trance and delusional reality that the religion drug can provide. The victim continues to practice the rituals of the religion and falls out of love with God and in love with the compulsion. The perverted faith looks good and feels good, but it is a counterfeit of a true love for and faith in God.[4]

Let me hasten to say, of course, that healthy faith is frequently accompanied by overwhelming waves of feeling, especially for some of us. Yes, the feelings do feel good, don't they? When they happen to us, we can accept them with gratitude—as gifts—as long as we don't mistake these feelings for the substance of faith.

But not all people are wired that way. It is quite possible to have a deep and abiding faith without ever being swept away on the tide of religious feeling. A low-key faith is not necessarily a second-class faith.

And so, for those whose emotions run high and for those whose don't, a caution: The feelings that often accompany faith are neither proof of faith nor the source of faith. But as my friend Jimmy used to say, "What really counts is not how high you jump or how loud you shout but the way you walk when you hit the ground!"

ROADBLOCK #2: SEEING IS BELIEVING

Second, as we indicated in the previous chapter, *faith is not knowledge*. Those who have to "see it to believe it" are missing the whole point of faith.

If we were sitting across the table from each other right now, I would hold up my closed fist and say, "Guess what I've got in my hand?" You might guess "a coin" or "keys" or whatever.

(Once as I did this during a speech, one little girl chimed out from the front row, "Air. You've got air in your hand." With an answer like that she couldn't lose. But then someone else sounded off, "No, the air is in his head, not his hand!")

At any rate, after you have guessed awhile, I might say to you, "I have a dollar bill in my hand. Do you believe that?" You might believe. You might not. But if you answered, "Yes. I believe that," you would "confess faith" that I was telling the truth.

In one sense, faith is trusting, upon the basis of reliable testimony, in that which cannot be seen. Or, as the Bible says, "Faith is being sure of what we *hope* for and certain of what we *do not see*."[5]

To further clarify this point, I might continue, "Now I am going to 'destroy' your 'faith.'" Then I would open my hand to show you the dollar bill. As soon as you laid eyes on it, you would no longer be merely a "believer"; you would be a "knower." Your faith would have become knowledge.

Knowledge, in this sense, can be validated by the five senses. But as we have said, we are not likely to see God in the way you could see my dollar bill. God transcends the senses and will not be subjected to empirical verification. That is why "we live by faith, not by sight."[6]

ROADBLOCK #3: YOU GOTTA BE GOOD

Third, *faith is not performance*. "Is" and "ought" remain poles apart in every life.

Does any person exist who didn't sin this week? Today? How about in the last hour? So, naturally, some of us talk ourselves down: "If I really were a genuine believer, I would be a better person." But flaws—even big flaws—are not necessarily evidence of the lack of faith.

One of the most compelling forces that keeps calling me back to God is the way Scripture seems zip-coded to my address. I feel as if Paul has been reading my mail when I read his anguished complaint:

> I do not understand what I do. For what I want to do I do not do, but what I hate I do.... I have the desire to do what is good, but I cannot carry it out. For what I do is not the good I want to do; no, the evil I do not want to do—this I keep on doing.... What a wretched man I am![7]

This is me exactly! You, too, right? The Bible identifies and analyzes our struggles with pinpoint accuracy: "There is no one righteous, not even one."[8]

Goodness and religious performance are not faith. And my rottenness is not evidence of a lack of faith. On the contrary, my inability to measure up is the very reason I must trust in the finished work of Jesus.

ROADBLOCK #4: IT'LL GET YOU OFF THE HOOK!

Faith is not the same thing as being good or righteous. But on the other hand, *faith is not a cop-out*. There is another brand of "pop faith" that must not be mistaken for genuine faith.

A nightclub singer I met in Houston graphically exhibited "cop-out religion." Her conversation was generously sprinkled with "Praise the Lord" and "Bless God." But she told me she did not have a husband because she did not need one; God supplied her with an endless string of husbands. "Why," she testified, "sometimes when I am singing, a man will walk into the club and the Holy Spirit will speak to my heart and say, 'That is the man you will sleep with tonight.'" Clearly this variety of "believing" does not honor a holy God!

Another person I met gushed, "I am so glad I have come to trust in the grace of God. Why, in the old days I used to be so guilt-ridden. Sometimes, after I had gotten drunk, picked up a woman, and taken her to bed, when all the passion was spent, I remember literally sitting on the edge of the bed and vomiting out of guilt.

> Faith is not an idea you hold but a dynamic reality that holds you.

But now that I have learned to trust in God's grace, I can go out and have a good time, guilt-free, no matter what happens!"

Flag this one: The messenger who announced, "By grace you have been saved, through faith,"[9] also warned, "Shall we go on sinning, so that grace may increase? By no means! We died to sin; how can we live in it any longer?"[10]

Yes, we are saved by biblical faith plus nothing. However, biblical faith is pretty inclusive and comprehensive stuff! It is not merely nodding to some abstract idea about God and then doing whatever we want to.

In the Bible, faith is not an idea you hold but a dynamic reality that holds you. For example, in the Gospel of John, faith is never a noun—it is always a verb. Faith moves. It does something. Faith not only affirms a new confession but forms a new creation.

Faith is trusting, all right, but that trust is unavoidably tied to turning—turning away from our old road and deliberately heading down God's road.

To put it in more traditional language, we cannot even believe without first repenting. Jesus made it quite explicit. "Repent," he said, "and believe the good news."[11]

56

ROADBLOCK #5: YOU HAVE TO GET IT RIGHT

Fifth, *faith is not correctness*. Real believers are not those who run the inside track with God because they get it all just right. The notion that faith equals correctness leads only to insecurity or self-righteousness, not to real faith.

If my standing with God depends upon the correctness of my doctrine, for instance, how can I ever be sure I am not wrong on some issue of eternal importance? And with that much at stake, how can I feel secure enough to keep on traveling the road of faith?

If, on the other hand, I manage to convince myself that I am right on every issue, what happens? My "correctness" mind-set breeds self-righteousness and its offspring, defensiveness and arguments. I end up planting my feet stubbornly in place instead of moving down the road.

Real faith means trust even in the midst of confusion as we continue to stumble toward the will of God. Repeated midcourse corrections will continue to redefine faith's understanding for a lifetime. But midcourse corrections, while they may align our walk more closely with the will of God, do not make us any more secure with Him. God already offers full security on the basis of our trust in Him and not our ability to totally understand Him.

ROADBLOCK #6: MANIPULATION IN THE NAME OF GOD

One brand of "faith" subtly attempts to use others—or even God—for its own ends. But *faith is not manipulation*.

James Gustafson said,

> My perception of a great deal of religious activity in the past two decades is that it is highly instrumental not for the purpose of honoring God and offering gratitude to Him, but for the purpose of inducing subjective states in human beings. If we can find some ways to make religion or God serve our ends (whether they be to help us feel better or to help us change the world for that matter) we use them; we use God for what we want.

I have wondered why, when certain people use God-language on me, I slip into my religion-proof vest. I may smile politely on the outside, but inside I silently hunt an escape route from the conversation.

No, I am not an atheist. Nor an agnostic. Nor do I despise public avowal of faith. Nevertheless, when someone comes on to me trying to get me "for God's sake" to buy a ticket or a book or a flag, or to support a candidate or a party or an issue—for some reason I dig in my heels.[12]

Could Gustafson have isolated a major source of cynicism? The person on the street gets hit too often by folks who try to use their religious beliefs as tools to achieve their own vested interests. We get the feeling that some actually believe God will play along with them!

In many instances, in fact, dodging counterfeit religious words may impede the flow of legitimate spiritual communication. Sometimes I find myself gun-shy of any sort of religious conversation, fearful that I may come off as a pious manipulator. Perhaps you find yourself experiencing the same thing.

We may profit from a fresh look at a very serious commandment: "Thou shalt not take the name of the LORD thy God in vain."[13] This commandment could literally be translated, "Do not use God's name for your own vain purposes." Too often, however, it has been twisted into a limp "folksism" that says, "Please don't cuss." Of course, I am not suggesting that cussing is a good thing. But using God's name for vain purposes may be an infinitely larger issue.

ROADBLOCK #7: DOUBTERS CAN'T HAVE FAITH

Finally, some think they don't have faith because they also *doubt*.

Carl and his wife, Marlene, were one of those couples everyone wanted to be like. They had fine kids and a beautiful home on the creek under the cottonwoods. At church, they had a special way of making everyone feel good. No one worked harder or seemed to care more. Carl and Marlene were usually the first ones there when someone was in need.

Then—wham! It all stopped. No one saw them at church for several weeks, and they began drifting out of touch with what was going on.

The Guilders, friends from church, stopped by one day to see them. Carl and Marlene greeted their guests with warmth, smiles, and refreshments. But in one of the awkward silences that fell after the preliminary superficial conversation, Carl said, "I know why you're here, of course. You care about us, and you know we have sorta dropped out."

"Yes, and we've missed you," acknowledged Jim Guilder. "We wondered if something was wrong."

"Not really," Carl replied in a lifeless tone. "It's just no use, that's all. I never will really have enough faith to be saved. Look, I never can do enough. So many times I have let really important things slide. And sometimes I feel angry at people and can't get over it. I even wonder about why God does things the way He does—if He does! *If a man really had faith he wouldn't feel this way.* I guess there is no way a man like me can be saved."

Like me and hundreds of others, Carl had convinced himself that he was not really a believer because he also had some doubts!

As this book will insist in several ways, *faith is not absence of doubt.* You will always be doing some doubting even while doing your best believing. Doubts do not destroy the meaning of your faith. Normal, healthy faith is often honeycombed with doubt, even at faith's more mature stages.

Remember, Ketar said, "I believe," but added, "help my *unbelief.*" Remember, also, my statement that doubt is not the same as unbelief. Doubt may lead to unbelief, and that is why it must be addressed, but the two, doubt and unbelief, are not necessarily equal.

Generally speaking, in the Bible, "unbelief" is much more concerned with disobedience, whereas "doubt" implies wavering between the two poles of belief and doubt—being "in two minds."[14] But these distinctions are not always clear; the meanings of the words translated "doubt" and "unbelief" overlap. Os Guinness explains:

There are times when the word *unbelief* is used to describe the doubts of those who are definitely believers but only when they are at a stage of doubting which is rationally inexcusable and well on the way to becoming full-grown unbelief (e.g. Luke 24:41). Thus the ambiguity in the biblical use of *unbelief* is a sign of psychological astuteness and not of theological confusion.[15]

It's not always easy to draw the line between doubt and unbelief. We may label our doubts as unbelief, for example, when we fear they are moving toward unbelief and aim to defeat them before that point is reached. Ketar appears to have done this—note that he said, "Help my *unbelief.*" Jesus, however, seems to see Ketar's struggle as what we commonly call doubt. He even responded to the man's cry as the prayer of a believer and healed Ketar's son.

Guinness goes on to say that what is important "is not that we know *when* doubt becomes unbelief (for only God knows this, and human attempts to say so can be cruel), but that we should be clear about *where* doubt leads to as it grows into unbelief."[16]

In other words, rather than our doubts condemning us, making us unbelievers, they may instead be encouraging us, making us hungry for more faith and spurring us on toward growth.

BUT WHAT *IS* FAITH?

These preceding pages are not meant to be a full catalog of distorted definitions. Many people are already believers but condemn themselves as doubters because they are blocked by one variety of "fantasy faith" or another: one crammed with warm fuzzies or empirically proven or fully understood or perfectly lived out or flooded with victory or stripped of doubt. In this chapter, I have simply attempted to clear the road to faith by pushing aside some of these misconceptions.

But did I hear someone say, "Okay, Lynn, we are getting a pretty good idea what faith is not. Enough of the negative! Just what is faith?"

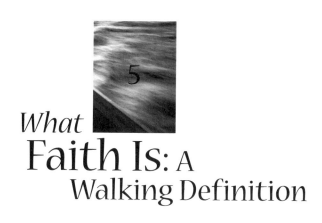

What Faith Is: A Walking Definition

The young seminarian had requested a private visit with the great preacher Charles Haddon Spurgeon. Behind closed doors the youth blurted out, "I fear I have lost my faith." Then he recited a litany of philosophical dilemmas, textual problems in Scripture, contradictions between science and the Bible, and a host of other issues he had encountered in his studies.

After listening to the catalog of quandaries, Spurgeon thundered, "Son, you haven't heard the half of it. Those doubts are child's play. When you have been a Christian as long as I, you'll confront such large doubts that little problems like these won't bother you at all."

Today, I draw comfort from that story, but it both frightened and frustrated me for quite a while, partly because it paralleled my own experience.

When I first began to come out of the "doubt closet" and timidly confess my "dark secrets," I was careful to approach only those I believed to be of deep piety, with superior intelligence and, above all, impeccable academic credentials. And their responses baffled me: While my confidants listened patiently, the ones I most respected showed no surprise over my questions and offered no "answers." Furthermore, they did not seem the least bit threatened either by my bulging bag of doubts or by their lack of answers.

This seemingly indifferent attitude triggered even more unnerving questions: *Is the whole of Christian leadership a vast conspiracy of cover-up?* I wondered. *Is the fraternity of Christian leadership, deep down, like the crowd who applauded the emperor's new clothes? Is each one only feigning belief because he or she wants to fit in with the others?*

A JOURNEY TO DISCOVERY

Then came that morning in October of 1966 when three of us crawled into an old Chevy and rolled out onto the Trans-Canada Highway from Kelowna, British Columbia, and headed east through the Canadian Rockies toward the Saskatchewan prairies. That long road twists through some mighty lonely country. For several hours, in fact, we drove out of range of radio stations. So we passed the time by taking turns at reading the Bible. We flipped it open at random and dived in at the Book of Romans.

For some reason, old verses took on fresh meaning that day. In the first three chapters we were sobered by the assessment that "all have sinned"[1] and that "all who sin…will be judged."[2] But then we hit more encouraging news: God cares! Because of His incredible love for us, He graciously sent Jesus. Through trust in Him, anyone can be saved.

My spirits soared. "Just think," I pondered, "there might even be hope here for someone like me. Maybe God really is on my side. All I need to do is simply put my life down on Him and trust Him to save me."

Maybe God really is on my side.

But the fourth chapter dashed my hopes: "Just believe—like Abraham!"

"So, that's the catch," I mused. "All we poor sinners need to do is just believe, huh? Like Abraham! Gimme a break! Me? Believe like Abraham? Who do you think I am?"

I felt myself sliding back into despair. In fact, as we rolled through the Rockies and I pondered what we had read, I actually began to feel angry at God.

Why, I had first met Abraham in my childhood Bible storybook. His face scowled from those pages in loud yellow, fringed by a ragged snow-white beard. Somber purple blotched his fearsome knuckles and streaked his otherworldly robe. In each picture Abraham stared gloomily at a purple sky that was splattered with a few yellow watercolor stars.

The Abraham of my memory was some weird, spiritual superman, a *Bible character*. But when I confessed this to my friend Stanley, he corrected me. "There aren't any Bible characters!" he chided. "All of those guys in the Bible are only people like you and me who just happened to be standing around when the Bible got written!"

That thought intrigued me! Abraham is called "the father of the faithful"—the walking definition of faith in both the Old and New Testaments. But he was not a Bible character, only a human being, like me. Perhaps, also like me, he stumbled through a ragged faith-career.

To think he was an equal—a fellow human being—making the same journey through life intrigued me. I had to know more about this man! So I thumbed back to Genesis and picked up on the father of the faithful where his story first intersects with Scripture.

Before I had read two verses, I stumbled onto a startling discovery about Abraham's faith!

Yes, Lord, But…

According to Genesis, the Lord called to Abraham, "Leave your country, *your people* and *your father's household* and go to the land I will show you." Then comes the revealing line: "So Abram left, as the LORD had told him; and *Lot went with him.*"[3]

Oops! Don't miss those last four words. The father of the faithful was told to go and to leave his kinfolks behind. And apparently he had enough faith to go. But not enough faith to go alone!

So, first rattle out of the box, father Abraham *disobeyed the Almighty.* He took his nephew along. In fact, he took his father part of the way, too, in spite of specific instructions not to.

While descending the eastern slopes from Kicking Horse Pass, I was considering an exciting possibility that seemed too good to be true. At first it was just a tentative question that I began to muse on: "Could a person actually believe and doubt at the same time?" Why, I can believe like that! Can you?

As just one example, I might trust God when He says it is more blessed to give than to receive. So I give—some—but I hold back some too. "I know God said it is more blessed to give, but just in case…!" I can be just generous enough that if God's principle turns out to be true, I might get some of the blessing. But I might also hoard some, too, so that my little cache may bring me blessing if God doesn't.

Sounds like Abraham's game! "Yes, Lord, I know you told me to head off across the country to some vague place, and to leave kin behind. Now, mind you, I will leave *most* of them behind. But couldn't I just take my dad and my nephew along?—only on the first leg of the journey, of course. Let me ease into this slowly, like getting into a tub of hot water. On the second leg of the trip, I'll just take the one nephew…."

Frankly, I do a great deal of that kind of "believing." How about you?

LAUGHING IN GOD'S FACE

As we follow his story farther, *Abraham literally laughed in God's face*. God blessed Sarah and said to Abraham, "I…will surely give you a son by her."[4]

And now, may I quote Abraham in a loose translation: "Haw, ah-ha, hee, hee, haw, haw…" More literally, he "fell face down; he laughed and said to himself, 'Will a son be born to a man a hundred years old? Will Sarah bear a child at the age of ninety?'"[5]

"Lord, you have to be joking!"

Now, this next question is not meant to be facetious, but do you know *anyone* who, upon hearing directly from God, has collapsed into fits of laughter over the absurd promises of the Almighty? Anyone?

Yes, I struggle a lot with doubts, but I cannot imagine laughing in God's face. Abraham did just that. What kind of faith is this?

I pondered the faith of the "father of the faithful" as we drove past Lake Louise. Somewhere west of Calgary, I began to realize, "Maybe I am not such a hopeless unbeliever, after all."

A FAILURE OF TRUST

But there is more to Abraham's story. I was stunned to discover that Abraham *trifled with the maid.*[6] Sarah, Abraham's wife, had born him no children. She said to Abraham, "Since the Lord has kept me from having children, go sleep with my maidservant, and maybe she will get pregnant."

Abraham did not protest, "Why, no, wife. That would be disobedience. And besides, God will keep His promise." One would expect the father of the faithful to say that! But, no. Abraham said, "Yes, ma'am," (my loose translation), and he went to bed with the maid! Then Sarah became jealous over the maid's pregnancy. She blamed Abraham. And she made life so miserable for Hagar that Hagar fled to the desert. Incredible as it sounds, Abraham wimped out and said, "Yes, ma'am, whatever you want," and helped Sarah drive the pregnant girl out toward starvation in the desert.

Abraham! I cannot believe you did that!

I have broken God's heart many times with my deep sins and rebellions, so I am not bragging about any goodness on my part. But I honestly have never done anything quite like what Abraham did!

Of course, Carolyn never has suggested that I sleep with the maid! Since we have four children, Carolyn and I have never been quite this desperate to have a baby! And in spite of myself, I cannot imagine encouraging Carolyn to drive a pregnant girl out into the wilderness to starve. So—am I more righteous than Abraham?

No, we cannot impose our New Testament mores on Abraham. Sleeping with the maid for the purposes of conceiving a child would not in itself be considered that big a deal in Abraham's day. You and I are shaped by a different set of cultural norms.

Nevertheless, Abraham committed industrial-strength sin! The shocker here is Abraham's *unbelief*.

On the one hand, Abraham believed God, but the years passed and no child of promise was born. So it appears that the father of the faithful began to doubt. Abraham and Sarah were getting pretty old for childbirth. Abraham seemed to think that by sleeping with the maid he would be helping God fulfill His promise. Abraham believed, all right, but disobedience and doubt also mingled with his faith. (Do you suppose he may even have wondered if Medicare covers pregnancy?) I can believe like that too. Can you?

A COWARD'S FAITH

We are still not finished with Abraham's strange story. In addition to what we have already mentioned, Abraham actually *loaned his wife* to another man.[7]

Sarah must have been a knockout in her seventies! Abraham was sure she was stunning enough that someone else might want her. In fact, when she and Abraham found themselves in Egypt, Abraham said to Sarah, "When the Egyptians see you, they will say, 'This is his wife.' Then they will kill me but will let you live." So, he told Sarah to "say you are my sister, so that I will be treated well for your sake."[8]

Abraham guessed right! Sarah caught the king's eye and landed in his harem. Consequently, God rained disease on Pharaoh's household. When Pharaoh sensed that the new woman in his house was bringing him this grief, he roared at Abraham, "Why didn't you tell me she was your wife?"[9]

This story blows my doors off! Here is a man with enough faith in God to dump his ranch and his relatives and head across country in search of some phantom promised place. Yet when he was backed against the wall, he actually loaned out his wife! Seems he was not sure God would protect him from Pharaoh's ruthless lust.

Why did Abraham do this? The answer has to be *doubt*. He was afraid—and fear is a form of unbelief. Abraham, like me and Ketar, believed but needed *help with his unbelief.* (Yes, Virginia, it *is* possible to experience faith and unbelief at the same time.)

FAITH AND UNCERTAINTY

And where did Abraham's faith-story take him in the long run? He draws a puzzling final comment in the New Testament. The author of Hebrews tells us that in following God, Abraham was "looking forward" not only to a new home and a son but also "to the city with foundations, whose architect and builder is God."[10] Abraham and other Old Testament people, from Abel to the prophets, "were still living by faith when they died."[11] And they "were all commended for their faith, yet none of them received what had been promised."[12]

> It is possible to believe and be an 'unbeliever' at the same time! The Bible says so!

This father of the faithful, in other words, didn't get all he expected out of his faith; he didn't receive all of what he believed God for. Although he did live to reach a new land and to see his promised son born, he was not around for the realization of everything God had promised him.

What are you telling us, Abraham?

Most of us were brought up to believe that having faith meant being so convinced in what we believe that all doubts are totally eradicated and thus all sinful behavior driven from life. Doesn't real faith mean we fear nothing? And doesn't faith mean that our prayers will be answered and we will get to see the results of our belief?

Maybe. But this surely isn't what faith meant for Abraham—nor for most of the faithful of the ages.

I closed the book on Abraham somewhere near Medicine, Alberta. By then I had begun to see with new eyes many things previously invisible to me. The words of Ketar invaded my confusion like a blinding shaft of sunlight stabbing into a dark cave—"Lord, I do believe, but help me *overcome my unbelief."*

Bingo! Dawn broke inside my soul as my internal question became an external affirmation: "It is possible to believe and be an 'unbeliever' at the same time! The *Bible* says so!"

THE STRUGGLE *IS* FAITH

The epic saga of Abraham, who is called no less than the "father of the faithful," reveals a near lifelong mixture of trust and fear, faith and doubt. And Abraham is not alone. On the return trip through the Rockies, I began to eagerly devour the many gripping tales of faith and doubt that unfold throughout the Bible. And I was stunned at the startling emotional honesty with which many of the Old Testament figures dared to challenge God Himself!

The Book of Job, for instance, follows no gentle story line. Instead, it catches us up in one man's staggering test of faith. Job was a good man, a faithful man. Brutal things happened to him, through no fault of his own. And Job did not accept his problems meekly. Rather he demanded, "I desire to speak to the Almighty and to argue my case with God."[13] In his last speeches, Job hits God with every example of injustice he can think of.

Don't rush to the end of Job's story and miss the impact of his painfully honest words. As Philip Yancey says, "One does not expect to find the arguments of God's greatest adversaries—say, Mark Twain's *Letters from the Earth* or Bertrand Russell's *Why I Am Not a Christian*—bound into the center of the Bible."[14] But there they are, minus Twain's and Russell's bylines! Although Job does hang in there with God, he refuses to skew the evidence or to whitewash what is clearly a bad situation.

What Philip Yancey noticed about Job's frankness toward God shows up often in the Scriptures. God's methods did not always meet with Jeremiah's approval either, for instance, and the prophet doesn't mind saying so: "I would speak with you about your justice: Why does the way of the wicked prosper? Why do all the faithless live at ease?"[15]

Even fiery John the Baptist doubted! John called into question the most central affirmation of his life with this skeptical question: "Are you the one who was to come, or should we expect someone else?"[16] And as Earl Palmer comments about John's question, "These are doubts that shake the world because they come from a man who had once been so certain of the world's foundation cornerstone."[17]

The stories of great believers—stretching from Abraham through Job through Ketar through doubting Thomas—shoot straight about the faith/doubt struggle. Possibly, even Jesus Himself gave us permission to anguish, even to doubt, when He cried out, "My God, my God, why have you forsaken me?"[18]

Like the fresh brilliance of the Saskatchewan dawn, this insight flooded me with a hopeful possibility: *Doubt is not all damnable.*

As my friend Andre Resner says, "The struggle with God is not lack of faith. It *is* faith!"[19] In fact, healthy faith contains plenty of healthy doubts! "Maybe I was not sick or warped or evil all those years of kicking rocks down my boyhood roads and rolling boulders up my manhood hills," I realized. "My faith may have been fairly normal!"

FAITH THAT DOESN'T GIVE UP

Be careful now! This saga is not suggesting that if you really want to get with God's program Abraham-style you should:

- disobey God
- laugh in the face of God's promises
- go to bed with the maid
- drive a pregnant woman out to the harsh wilderness
- or loan your wife to a lecherous king

Obviously not! No, the idea is not to imitate Abraham's *short-comings* but to gain clearer understanding of faith from Abraham's *doubts!*

But don't hurry away. There is one more major thing to learn from Abraham. *Faith may doubt, but it doesn't give up.*

Abraham believed God. Once he stopped laughing, he believed

God could produce a son even in his and Sarah's advanced years. He believed God would give him a new home, a new place to settle. On the basis of God's promises, Abraham decided—and moved out.

He believed God strongly enough that in spite of his fears and misgivings, when God said go, Abraham got going. He picked up his left foot and set it down in front of his right foot with his toes pointed in the direction of the unseen land. Then he set his right down in front of the left. And Abraham kept picking them up and setting them down. He kept on walking. And walking. And walking.

Abraham kept on walking even when there seemed little evidence that he was going anywhere.

Imagine what was going on in Abraham's heart all this time. He must have experienced periods of overwhelming doubt, fear, and even feelings of rebellion—but he didn't stop. What an enormous struggle of the will Abraham must have exercised just to keep on putting one foot in front of the other!

Abraham kept on walking even when there seemed little evidence that he was going anywhere.

Surely Abraham must have wondered, "Ah, come on now. Where is this baby son God promised to a ninety-year-old woman and a hundred-year-old man? Why, years have passed since God said that, and no kids play around my tent. Besides, I've been traveling for nearly a lifetime, and I haven't even arrived at any destination."

But Abraham kept on walking!

Do you suppose, as the years and the miles rolled by, that Abraham pondered, "Am I sure about the night God promised me all this? That was a long time ago. Did I really hear Him correctly? Did I really hear anything at all? Maybe I just ate too much lamb and garlic before I went to bed that night and dreamed up all this stuff!"?

Could Abraham have gone so far as to ask himself, as you and I may have asked, "Is God really there at all? If He's there, is He able to produce what He promised? Or has He forgotten me?"

But in spite of his doubts, Abraham kept setting one foot in front of the other. Up and down. He kept on walking. Throughout his life he kept following the initial decision he had made to believe God, and the Bible says God "credited it to him as righteousness."[20]

God did not call Abraham righteous on the basis of Abraham's ability to know right, to feel right, to do right, or to be doubt-free. Instead, God credited righteousness to Abraham's account because Abraham never gave up on his relationship with God.

Abraham chose to trust God and thus head in God's direction despite the times he wavered in doubt. And God honored that. He did not seem to be nearly as interested in the distance Abraham had come or the speed he was traveling as in the direction he was headed and the fact that he kept on going.

Perseverance. Surely that is what God wants from us too!

Faith's Bottom Line

So this brings us to the bottom line: What is faith, Abraham-style?

Faith is, at its heart, a commitment of the will. It is a choice made in favor of God, a decision of the will to keep on moving in a Godward direction. It is perseverance in spite of the obstacles that doubt may throw in the way.

When we examine the story line of all faithful figures in the Bible, we find that the taproot of their faith is the same. Faith begins with a decision that keeps on being made, day after day, to trust God. One step at a time. No matter what!

However, making a "decision of the will" does not mean that we can steel our spines and "accomplish" great faith. Instead, it means that we surrender our own wills to God. We choose to head in God's direction. To take the winding road that He points out. In other words, the validity of our faith does not lie in the strength of our wills but in the One we choose to trust.

The free choice of the human will in the presence of God's sovereignty presents a great mystery. I do not know why one person will choose to trust and another will not.

For example, I know a pair of identical twins who grew up in the same home. They were exposed to the same external influences and the same parenting. One of them chose to trust God and is a man of great character and vast positive influence. His life has borne a lot of spiritual fruit. The other twin chose his own devious ways and is a physical, ethical, and spiritual wreck. Why? Who knows. Each of us can be responsible only for our own choices.

And the choice, again, is totally up to us. The Bible says so very clearly: "The Spirit and the bride say, 'Come!' And let him who hears say, 'Come!' Whoever is thirsty, let him come; and whoever wishes, let him take the free gift of the water of life."[21]

From God's perspective, faith is a gift. From our human perspective, faith begins with a choice, a *decision of the will*. And our faith grows as we move out and keep on choosing faith—or at least choosing to *want* faith—even when there appears to be no reason for believing.

KEEP ON WALKING

Your faith may be honeycombed with doubts, especially at certain periods of the journey. That's all right. Don't call yourself an unbeliever because sometimes you don't feel like a believer. Or because you have doubts in your heart. Or because you messed up—royally.

Instead, keep on walking. Set your will. Keep on trusting. Yes, fan that tiny spark of faith into a roaring flame. Feed that fire any way you can. Don't back away from it.

At times it will seem, "If I turn to Christlike living, I might miss some of life's gusto." Forget it, keep on walking.

"But you don't know what I did last Saturday night. I must not have much faith, or I wouldn't have done that." Get up and keep on walking. If you can't walk, then crawl. It is better to crawl in God's direction than to give up.

"I have tried so hard and so long to learn how to love people, but I still seem so full of bitterness. I'm wondering if God's promises are true—at least for me." Keep on walking. Don't quit.

It takes very little faith to take the first step, so take it now! He will walk with you from there, lift you up when you fall, and carry you when your strength is gone. That is good news! When we don't trust ourselves, we can trust Him! So even in times when we blow it or doubt it or don't feel anything, we can just keep going, keep walking into His will. That's faith!

Don't throw up your hands and say, "Phooey. I guess I don't believe. I'll just give up, and that's it." This is precisely what Satan wants you to do when doubt hits. But God knows how you feel. Through Abraham and the whole cast of the biblical drama, God is saying, "I understand how you feel. I really do. But don't quit! The father of the faithful had his peculiar problems too, but he kept on walking."

Dogwood, a musical group out of Nashville, recorded a song some time back that underscores this walking definition of faith:

Are you weary in well doing
Walkin' on the road to New Jerusalem?
Are you hopin' and a prayin'
Lookin' any minute for the Lord to come?
And do you see a lot of pleasant lookin' places
Where you might lay down and take a rest?
And if you do take a look at all the faces there
The sadness will tell you that it's best
To…
Keep on walkin'—you don't know how far you've come.
Keep on walkin'—for all you know it may be done
And the Father might be standin' up right now
To give a call—and end it all—so keep on walking.[22]

But how do you take the first step? How does faith come? Let's now consider the steps in our journey of faith.

.

PART 3

I Sort of Believe,
but Why Is My
Faith Different
from Yours?

"How can you believe if you accept praise
from one another, yet make no effort
to obtain the praise that comes from the only God?"

—JOHN 5:44

Stages of the Journey

All along my journey of faith, periodic doubt has nipped at my heels. Yet most of the time I have also craved wholehearted belief in the God of my father and involvement in the family of God. Nurtured from childhood in the embrace of a tiny, close-knit Christian fellowship, I depended on the church for much of my security and identity. Yet all the time I wondered, *Would they accept me if they knew I do not truly believe?*

Through the rearview mirror, I see that much of what I called "unbelief" was not really that at all. I wasn't really an unbeliever; I just didn't believe everything my community of faith expected me to. Nor did I believe with the same simplicity and intensity I saw in people whose faith I respected.

Back then, however, I felt increasingly troubled over what I saw as a lack of integrity on my part. Was I a hypocrite, professing belief on the outside while harboring serious doubts on the inside? I craved the approval of my believing circle, so I learned to bide my questions, but I was eaten up with guilt over my masquerade.

Then I made three pivotal discoveries that helped me give up the guilt and get moving again on the road to faith.

The first two we have already examined:

First, I began to understand that doubting is a part of healthy faith.

Second, I learned that faith, at root, is a decision of the will, not a feeling or an accomplishment.

And then I made what was for me—and has been for many others before me—a pivotal discovery: *Mature faith usually doesn't happen all at once, and it does not have to look exactly alike in all believers.* Like physical and emotional development, faith normally grows through a series of predictable stages, yet preserves personal uniqueness at the same time.

For a few fortunate people, faith appears to happen all at once—in a flash of insight, an arresting conversion experience, an existential leap, or the like. But it doesn't work that way for most of us.

Mature faith usually doesn't happen all at once, and it does not have to look exactly alike in all believers.

And closer examination may reveal that even these "instant believers" grow through stages of development. Some may zip through at such a pace they would hardly call them stages. Others may simply not have been aware of the processes at work during various phases of faith development.

At any rate, faith for most of us is a matter of beginning at some point and moving on from there.

I noticed this "developmental principle" first from literature in the field of developmental psychology. Then I began to notice that the Bible supports it as well. The apostle Peter, for instance, said that we begin in the faith as "newborn babes" who "crave pure spiritual milk, so that by it [we] may *grow up* in [our] salvation."[1] Paul celebrated, "We ought always to thank God...because [our] *faith is growing* more and more."[2]

This, of course, is another reason our friend Ketar could say, "I do believe, but could you *help my unbelief?*" But as incredible as this now seems, I had not known that growing through stages of faith is normal and healthy. Consequently, I had labeled all my doubts as "unbelief" and all my vacillation and questions as "evil" at worst, or "instability" at best. I had not needed to walk those peaks and valleys with such a sense of hopelessness.

Imagine my excitement as insight from developmental psychology and strong signals from Scripture were further confirmed by current literature on faith development. All of these told me my own experience was fairly normal. Where doubt had kicked rocks, faith now bloomed like the crocuses.

Possibly you will resonate with me. Maybe you, too, will personally identify with these specific seasons of growing faith and find them helpful.

Numerous writers have helped me explore the stages of faith and their implications for our times of doubt. James Fowler, building on Erik Erickson, maps out six distinct stages of faith development. Janet Hagberg and Robert Guelich describe four stages, then a "wall," and then add two more stages. Sharon Parks and several others add further dimension to the concept of faith development.[3]

None of these descriptions of faith development is the "correct" one; each is simply a paradigm, a way of seeing. For the purposes of this book, I will follow John Westerhoff's lead and picture faith development as occurring in four stages:[4]

- faith's infancy
- faith's childhood
- faith's adolescence
- faith's adulthood

FAITH'S INFANCY

Faith is first "experienced" before it is actually chosen, says Westerhoff.[5] Using Westerhoff's terminology, I envision the first stage of faith development as the infancy of faith—when a person does not have faith but rather experiences the faith of others.

A child born into a family of believers first feels faith's hugs and hears "God-talk" as part of the fabric of his or her family life. At bedtime, childhood faith prays, "Now I lay me down to sleep" or sings "Jesus Loves Me" as it has been taught. At this stage, even very healthy "experienced faith" basically only basks in the glow of other people's faith.

However, while infant faith is often experienced at biological babyhood, this is not always so. For example, a seventy-five-year-old unbeliever may spend his late years in the home of a Christian daughter and her family and experience faith for the first time in old age. And although at some point he may even appear to believe all at once, in reality he has moved through a spiritual infancy before coming to faith.

Experienced faith is a natural and healthy doorway to belief. However, it is not robust, mature faith. Healthy faith development, like healthy physical or psychological development, doesn't stop at infancy but grows and changes, moving toward maturity.

FAITH'S CHILDHOOD

After infancy comes the childhood of faith, which of course does not necessarily come during biological childhood. At this stage, the person believes certain things because he or she is affiliated with a group of people who believe such things. Westerhoff labels this stage "affiliative" faith.

Affiliative faith is the faith of a teenager who spouts church dogma, although she would scarcely be able to explain why she believes it. Or when faith's childhood occurs during biological adulthood, it may involve enthusiastic denominational loyalty, memorized and recited Scripture, unquestioning acceptance of congregational rules. And it definitely involves embracing the group's assumptions about what constitutes faith.

Affiliative faith, like experienced faith, is a normal stage on the road of faith development, providing we don't park there. Scripture warns specifically against getting stuck in faith's childhood.

> By this time you ought to be teachers, you need someone to teach you the elementary truths of God's word all over again. You need milk, not solid food!... But solid food is for the

mature, who by constant use have trained *themselves* to distinguish good from evil.[6]

Don't let the slightly different metaphor (the infant term) throw you here; the author of Hebrews was speaking directly to those whose spiritual development becomes arrested at the *affiliative* level, those who still depend on others around them to tell them what to believe.

Faith stalled out at this point becomes fragile and defensive. It dodges intellectual examination and often cannot cope with alternative viewpoints; thus it tends to turn inward toward sectarianism and isolationism.

That was what happened to Amy.

At seventy years of age, Amy knew "the truth." She was sure of it. She wasn't mean or argumentative—not even self-righteous. But she belonged to a congregation that represented the very narrowest wing of a very narrow denomination. And she just couldn't think outside her religious categories. It was too dangerous. She might get confused. She might swallow some doctrinal error. So she avoided people who thought differently than she did. That was easy, because all of her friends and her family belonged to her denomination and held staunchly for "the truth" as well.

But then Amy wound up in the hospital. And shortly after she got there, she called for her cousin, Clarence, who was a minister in her denomination. She said she had something terribly important to discuss with Clarence and no one else.

Clarence slid into a chair by the bed and picked up Amy's hand. Her hand trembled, and anxiety spelled itself all over her face.

"What is it, Cousin Amy?"

"Oh, Clarence. It's awful. I didn't mean any harm by it, and he was such a nice man. But I needed you to come and let me ask you if I did the right thing!"

"What *is* it, Cousin?"

"Well, you know they have a new minister down at the Episcopal church, and he seems like such a kind young man. He visits everybody in the hospital, not just his members. Well, you know Episcopalians don't believe like we do. In fact, they don't believe much at all, as far as I can tell. But, Clarence, that young man asked me if he could say a word of prayer for me, and—Clarence, *I went ahead and let him!* What does our church teach? Can I get forgiveness for that?"

Of course, affiliative faith may be less narrow than Amy's. People in more "open" denominations go through this stage of faith as well, and they, too, may become arrested in their development.

In addition, people at this faith stage may not necessarily buy in to the particulars of a group's faith as heavily as Amy did. In fact, some "affiliative believers" privately reject part of what the group believes while publicly going along. I did. And although it is very important to them that they belong, they think of themselves as unbelievers or skeptics because they don't believe all of what the group believes. A painful internal duplicity may result.

It may be more accurate to say that by the time a person begins to feel this way, he or she has actually become a closet adolescent—no longer in the affiliative stage. Possibly. But that may be too simple an explanation. A person may be feeling the first twinges of adolescent or searching faith yet at the same time still be primarily at the affiliative stage.

Westerhoff's categories are not meant to be quite so clear-cut. In reality, a person may gravitate back and forth between stages or may actually be in two stages at one time. Faith may be affiliative in one area of personality while it is at its adolescent, or searching stage, in another.

And that partially explains why, as a twelve-year-old boy who found some dimensions of my childhood God unbelievable, I loathed my "unbelief" as I kicked rocks down my road. Yet what I called unbelief was actually the first twinges of faith's adolescence. I was having trouble believing what affiliative faith seemed to expect. I was no longer satisfied with the group answers. I had to discover faith for myself.

Faith's Adolescence

Our son Jon, who was thirteen years old, had something on his mind. While we drove, he fiddled with the edge of his seat cover. Then, sucking in a deep breath, he asked, "Dad, what if our church is wrong?"

"Why do you ask?"

"You know. Our church reads the Bible. And some of my friends at school read the Bible in their churches too—but they believe different from us. What if we are wrong?"

"Well, bud, I disagree with our church on some points myself."

"That's confusing. How do you know what is right then, Dad?"

"There is no such thing as a church that is right, son; none of us have a corner on truth. But remember who is right. Jesus is 'the way, the truth, and the life.' His word is true. So always trust what the Bible says and follow Jesus—no matter what the church says."

The adolescence of faith may be painful.

"But what if that leads me out of our church?"

"That could happen. If you can't follow Jesus and honor the Bible in our church, it could mean our church has gotten too far off the track. In that case, you may need to leave...*if* you leave to follow Jesus. Remember, though, you may see some things 'wrong,' no matter what church you become a part of."

A long pause followed. "Oh, well. I'll probably just stay in our church."

What was happening in this exchange? Jon was flashing early signals of his move to the next stage of faith's development: adolescence. Of course, at the end of that particular conversation he put further exploration temporarily on hold. And countless biologically adult church members stop permanently where Jon did and never progress further.

Stages one and two are part of healthy faith development provided, of course, that one does not get stuck in them. But growing faith must move on through adolescence. And get ready, because the adolescence of faith may be painful.

Bill Cosby dubbed *biological* adolescence as "temporary brain damage." I understand why. When our first child hit the ninth grade, Carolyn and I felt sure that she was mentally ill—or we were. We kissed a sweet, compliant, and cuddly child to sleep one night and woke the next morning to find a sullen and capricious alien in our house.

Of course, I am being facetious, and this adolescent caricature is unfair. But many a parent of teenagers would swear it's true—and their children would have equally scary stories to tell. Every child's experience of adolescence is different, but adolescence is frightening to both parent and child. Still, wise parents know that adolescence is a healthy developmental stage that actually ushers children into the world of adults.

Spiritual adolescence is very real too. And like its biological counterpart, spiritual adolescence can be terrifying. Westerhoff calls spiritual adolescence "searching faith" because during this time we examine, even challenge, our affiliative faith. And like its biological counterpart, spiritual adolescence often brings experimentation and confrontation.

However, spiritual adolescence may not coincide with biological adolescence. (My own certainly didn't; although I felt early tweaks, it didn't really hit me with full force until I had been in the ministry for several years.) It may strike at fifteen or fifty.

During this period, typically, questions swarm: Why do Christians believe that? Is the Bible reliable? Why does God do this—or allow that? Is God really a loving God?

These questions often worry or threaten parents and church leaders. Some overreact. "Don't ask those troubling questions. They upset people. Are you trying to be difficult?" The questioner may get labeled as a troublemaker—or even as an unbeliever.

How unfortunate! Quite often the strident challenges of adolescent faith are actually healthy signs—a mark of spiritual vitality.

What on the surface appears to be an attitude problem may actually be an essential rite of passage into more mature faith.

During this unsettling stage of faith, it can be comforting to know that the Bible provides support for searching faith. Smack in the middle of the Book of Acts, applause breaks out for the folks at Berea. They were "more noble" than their neighbors because they "examined the Scriptures every day to see if what Paul said was true."[7]

Wise spiritual leaders know that tough questions and challenges become doorways to growth when they are nurtured by a circle of listening ears, informed minds, and caring hearts. If, however, at this crucial stage of faith, questioning gets squashed, the searcher may feel driven to one of at least three negative options.

1. Getting Out. The muzzled questioner may simply walk out of his or her church or family and head down the street to where questions are welcomed (or just ignored). These days, in fact, sincere searchers are leaving in droves from fearful, rigid churches, and "high control" families often shatter.

2. Staying Mad. Stymied faith can settle into chronic anger. Some silenced searchers can neither quiet their questions nor summon the courage to leave. So they simply get mad and stay mad, either swallowing their ball of rage or aiming it at unrelated issues. Some chronically unhappy people hang around the church for a lifetime, constantly embroiled in conflict or venting their anger in more subtle, sometimes unconscious ways. Some angry people even gain positions of prominence. You may know a minister who, at midlife, still nurses anger, his or her ministry leaving a trail of trouble.

3. Turning off the Questions. This is the most deadly choice of all. The seeker may simply ignore the questions, join the crowd, and pretend to believe like everyone else. This person must become expert at turning off anything really thought-provoking, lest the questions get stirred up again. But tabling the big questions at faith's adolescent stage is a dangerous habit and can lead gradually to the dismantling of both integrity and conscience. A person who turns off the questions may eventually wind up unable to believe very intensely in anything.

The only bridge from childhood to adulthood is adolescence. If we are to grow, we must cross it and ask our questions, even if they challenge longstanding comfort zones. If not, while we may say God-words and maintain religious identity, our faith will lack vitality; for all practical purposes, we will live as if we believed in nothing.

Two words of caution are necessary about searching faith: First, for those who may be tempted to blame their faithlessness on repressive churches or parents—the *search ultimately becomes the lonely responsibility of the searcher.* Many great believers of the centuries hammered out their faith on the anvil of suppression: Jeremiah, Luther, Stephen, and Jesus—to name a few. Encountering resistance is no excuse for failing to grow up spiritually.

> If we let reasonable doubts linger indefinitely, they can make us spiritual hypochondriacs— or perpetual adolescents!

Second, *searching faith has a dark side—the same old problem of arrested development.* The searcher may slip into a holding pattern, forever circling, never landing, and thus effectively avoiding responsibility.

Richard confides, "Sometimes I have been paranoid of closing my options, using the excuse that 'after all, if I don't know what to believe, I certainly cannot be expected to make any costly commitments.' The last thought to spin through my head before giving in to some favorite temptation was, 'Oh, well, what difference does it make? I'm likely not really a Christian anyway!'"

The apostle James seems to have had Richard in mind when he wrote, "He who doubts is like a wave of the sea, blown and tossed by the wind…. He is a double-minded man, unstable in all he does."[8] And Lois Cheney scores a direct hit on Richard's mentality in *God Is No Fool:*

> I once knew a young man who was searching for God. And I

was touched by his search; and I prayed for his search; and I loved his search.

He read a lot of books. He thought and thought about their ideas. He talked to many people, in pairs and in groups; they matched their minds with his and they furthered his search. He walked and sought God in the rain. He climbed and sought God on the mountain. He closed himself off from the world and sought God in his soul.

He would describe his searchings and travels for truth. He would explain how he had meticulously and prayerfully sorted, rejected, and accepted.

As the years went on I changed from anticipating the recounting of his searches, to simply receiving them; to being bored with them; to avoiding them; and him. You see, he had fallen in love with his search.

God just isn't that hard to find![9]

Beware of arrested development that cleverly maintains adolescent options and dodges the responsibilities of commitment by prolonging the search. The Bible says that some people are "always learning but never able to acknowledge the truth."[10] If we let reasonable doubts linger indefinitely, they can make us spiritual hypochondriacs—or perpetual adolescents!

Faith's Adulthood

Who knows exactly when a child becomes an adult? But that unseen line is eventually crossed. Likewise, healthy adolescent faith eventually moves into faith's adulthood.

Westerhoff labels the latter stages of faith as "owned" faith. At faith's adulthood, one is now coming to own a faith upon which he or she can build a life. However, entering the adult season of faith does not mark the end of search and growth.

This stage of growing, searching, yet maturing faith is characterized by several earmarks, as described by Peter Benson and Carolyn Eklin in their report on faith patterns:

1. Trusts in God's saving grace and believes firmly in the humanity and divinity of Jesus.
2. Experiences a sense of personal well-being, security, and peace.
3. Integrates faith and life, and sees work, family, social relationships and political choices as part of religious life.
4. Seeks spiritual growth through study, reflection, prayer, and discussion with others.
5. Seeks to be part of a community of believers in which people witness to their faith and support and nourish one another.
6. Holds life-affirming values, including...a personal sense of responsibility for the welfare of others.
7. Advocates social and global change [out of compassion for all human beings].
8. Serves humanity consistently and passionately through acts of love and justice.[11]

This growing adult faith may leave or remain in the denomination of its childhood. But whatever its outward affiliation, it clings less and less to the dogma and mores of a group, and more and more to a personal relationship with God. And even as owned faith becomes more comfortable with ambiguity and mystery, it may at the same time grow tougher and more resilient.

Paul the apostle is exhibit A. Imagine how different the course of history might have been had Paul not moved from affiliative faith through his own spiritual adolescence and into his owned faith! His faith became less dogmatic and more internalized at the same time. For example, Paul defended the right of Gentile believers to remain uncircumcised when his old buddies would have demanded it.[12] He championed the freedom of salvation by grace through faith rather than by works of the law.[13] He also stood up for all who could be disenfranchised on the basis of race, class, or sex: "There is neither Jew nor Greek, slave nor free, male nor female, for you are all one in Christ Jesus."[14]

Faith never completely outgrows dark valleys where it groans with Ketar, "Help my unbelief!" Reaching the stage of owned faith does not mean all questions are answered or that all views are correct or that all doubts vanish.

Remember, discovering faith is like finding a road, not a parking spot; it is not a quick or final fix.

In fact, a friend of mine recently tuned me in to a faith phenomenon I had not noticed, although it seems to hit a number of believers just after midlife and rings true for me. They may have walked in communication with God for a lifetime, with ever-richer faith. Then suddenly the line goes dead, as if God had hung up on them. They no longer "feel" God or "hear" God. Some feel panicky, thinking they have lost their faith.

But my friend pointed out that those times when God seems silent or distant may simply be times when we already have what we need from Him. When He gives no new light or new experience for a time, He means for us to act on what we know, on what He has taught us already. If we continue to move on, trusting in our experience of what He has done for us, we will eventually "hear His voice" again.

I do not see adult faith so much as a final stage but as the point where faith comes to terms with a development that lasts a lifetime. In the words of E. C. Roehlkepartain,

> It is a never-ending process with seasons of tremendous growth and times of near stagnation. At times God seems to direct every step we take, and at other times He feels as distant as another solar system.[15]

And yet the passage into spiritual adulthood is significant. It marks the point at which faith becomes internalized, the point where the believer can say, "This is my faith, and on it I put down my life." Or in Paul's words, "I know whom I have believed, and am convinced that he is able to guard what I have entrusted to him."[16] Once we reach that point on the journey of faith, our up-and-down journey takes on a completely new flavor.

Showdown with Integrity

The journey of growing faith is uneven. It can be exhilarating and at times painful—and reaching maturity doesn't mean you have arrived.

But the alternative to a lifetime of growth can be disastrous. If we don't continue to grow, we may jeopardize our integrity, if not our faith itself.

When I was kicking rocks down the roads of my childhood, I thought I was a hypocrite. But had I chosen to stop growing at that point, even at that tender age, my integrity would already have been compromised.

Stephen Crane, author of the famous novel *The Red Badge of Courage*, confronted the pain of integrity in his poem "The Wayfarer":

> The wayfarer,
> Perceiving the pathway to truth,
> Was struck with astonishment.
> It was thickly grown with weeds.
> "Ha," he said,
> "I see that none has passed here
> In a long time."
> Later he saw that each weed
> Was a singular knife.
> "Well," he mumbled at last,
> "Doubtless there are other roads."[17]

Perhaps Stephen Crane was describing himself. (Not long after this poem was written, and at a very young age, he committed suicide.) Or perhaps he is telling the story of all who fear the sharp intruding edges that cut away faith's childhood and goad us toward owned faith and beyond.

This showdown with integrity frightens us. But for many of us, healthy faith cannot—repeat, *cannot*—develop without it.

Jesus warned against the dangers of packaging faith for the prevailing market: *"How can you believe* if you accept praise from one another, yet make no effort to obtain the praise that comes from the only God?"[18] Jesus, am I hearing you correctly? Are you saying that real faith may be impossible if we "go along" just to "get along"; if we abandon our search and smother our consciences in order to keep the peace or to keep our options open or, worse still, to gain acceptance and praise?

THE CHILL WINDS OF OPPOSITION

The mercury had dipped to thirty below on that Canadian February day in 1936 when the rough hands of hardy homesteaders lugged a cattle trough up the hill and shoved it through the door into my mother's kitchen. Then they carried buckets of water from the well, heated it on our coal-fed stove, poured it into the trough, and baptized my mother and father, sealing a decision that had been made a year earlier. My parents put their trust in Jesus and took responsibility for the implications of their own faith.

But Mom and Dad were laughed out of their social circle for a time, because they dared to leave affiliative security in order to embrace their owned faith. While this pained them deeply, they could do nothing else with integrity. Mom and Dad's faith development would have come to a screeching halt had they ignored their questions, swallowed their doubts, and silenced their consciences.

> Jesus warned against the dangers of packaging faith for the prevailing market.

In moments of introspection, I am puzzled by my own attitudes: Why do I so admire my parents' courage yet get antsy when my children (walking in the heritage of their grandparents) sometimes own conclusions that don't match mine? Would I want to steer my children away from the integrity that I so much admire in my mom and dad? Would I want my kids to settle permanently on the theological turf that my pilgrim parents saw only as frontier?

Of course, I do believe some things deeply enough that I want my children to share them. But I don't want them to quell their consciences to please me. Yet I pray that they will love God enough to pursue Him even if that search drives them out of any ruts I am following and leads them in directions that break my heart.

Merle Crowell tells a story about a Greenland Eskimo who joined an American Arctic expedition. For his faithful guide service he was rewarded with a visit to New York City. Dazzled by the wonders, he couldn't wait to tell the folks back home in Greenland. He described "stacks of igloos that reached the clouds" and "crowded igloos moving along the trail" and "lamps that burned without seal oil."

But the village people did not share his excitement. Instead, they listened with fish-eyed stares, tagged him "Sagdluk" (that is "The Liar"), and shunned him, By the time of his death, his original name had long been forgotten, and he carried the name *Liar* to his grave.

Later, Knud Rasmussen made his trip to Alaska, guided by another Greenland Eskimo named Mitek. Mitek, too, was rewarded with a trip to New York. Although he was dazzled by the city, Mitek, remembering Sagdluk's fate, covered his backside by cooking up stories that his villagers could swallow. He and Rasmussen had only "paddled a big kayak on a wide river called Hudson, among plentiful flocks of geese and large herds of seals."[19]

Thus, Mitek, who was the real liar, gained a place of extraordinary respect among his home villagers. The man who had told the real truth was called Liar and died in ignominy.

But this should not surprise us. Those hardy souls who exercise the freedom to pursue truth often face such a chill wind. Remember Jeremiah in the well? And Stephen being stoned? Luther at the Council of Worms? My parents and possibly yours? Most especially, remember Jesus on the cross. Can we expect to obtain freedom of conscience through some ecclesiastical fiat? Will humankind one day automatically reward such integrity?

I doubt it! But nonetheless, each of us is as free as all truth seekers have been from Jeremiah to Sagdluk—provided that we, like they, value authentic faith highly enough to maintain the payments. Washington cannot provide integrity by legislation. The church or seminary cannot guarantee freedom of thought through some ingenious movement. Freedom is in the heart.

Those who best pursue God do so even in the face of a hostile environment. To them, a relationship with Christ means more than keeping a job or holding an audience or receiving accolades from their fellows (though all these may be precious). They seem strangely hungry for "the praise that comes from the only God"— the fresh breeze of freedom that comes only from refusing to get stuck on the road of faith.

WHERE ARE YOU IN THE JOURNEY?

Where is your faith? Can you place your finger on the precise point of progress in your own faith development?

Are you beginning to wonder if your faith is simply a reflection of the group with which you are affiliated? No rush. No panic. You have some growing to do—but so do most people. Paul the apostle was an old man before he wrote, "I know whom I have believed…."

Or do you feel unsettled, confused, doubting more than you are believing? Remember, doubts need not pigeonhole you as an unbeliever, and your questions need not categorize you as a rebel. They are mileposts on the road that leads to faith's maturing adulthood.

But ask yourself: How long have you been searching? For decades? If you find the endless theoretical discussion is a fun ego massager and you secretly dread the closing of your options, be careful. Your well-fed doubt may really be a cop-out, and it may be time for you to move on. Do not be afraid to break out of your holding pattern and resume your flight plan!

If you are feeding your faith and it is beginning to shape your life, you are showing signs of owned faith. But if you are also still experiencing periods of doubt, confusion, or just "flatness"…

Great! Sounds normal.

In actuality, your faith will likely slide all over the developmental landscape for as long as you live. One area of life might still be playing in faith's childhood while another marches into adulthood and another is wrestling with searching issues. Some of us find ourselves moving back and forth between stages of faith, searching awhile, then reverting to affiliative faith, and back and forth. And don't forget: Even mature, owned faith keeps on searching and sometimes cycling through periods of doubt.

Perhaps I will be a doubter all my life. But I am a believer too. After more than forty years of faith, I know far too few answers and I sometimes betray my own ideals. And yet somehow, from somewhere, I keep finding enough faith to go on.

How? Usually, I only have enough faith for one day at a time. Every morning as I roll out of bed, I make the conscious decision to trust God another day. And each day God gives me just enough faith, just as He gives each day enough sunlight. And I remain determined to cling to the One whom I cannot see, to follow a path I often do not understand, and to trust even if my whole world is caving in. My experience is something like that of M. Louise Haskins, who reflected,

> And I said to the man who stood at the gate of the year,
> "Give me a light, that I may tread safely into the unknown!"
> And he replied: "Go out into the darkness and put your hand into the Hand of God.
> This shall be to you better than a light and safer than a known way."
> So, I went forth, and finding the Hand of God, trod gladly into the night.
> And He led me toward the hills and the breaking of day in the lone East.[20]

Where then do I go from here to move forward in my journey of faith? Read on...

PART 4

I Believe,
but How
Can My Faith
Grow?

*Five Practical Steps
toward Stronger Faith*

*"If anyone chooses to do God's will,
he will find out whether my teaching comes
from God or whether I speak on my own."*
—JOHN 7:17

"Help me overcome my unbelief!"
—MARK 9:24

INTRODUCTION

Five More Steps on the Journey

In the next five chapters of this book, we will walk through five practical steps down the road toward a stronger faith. Sam Shoemaker first pointed me toward these ideas years ago through his book *Extraordinary Living for Ordinary Men*.[1] In the decades since, I have further hammered these out through my own experience—adding, subtracting, and revising—till my thoughts now bear only a hint of Shoemaker's influence. I want to acknowledge Shoemaker for his help, although he might not want to be held responsible for where I have gone with it.

In some ways, I hesitate to list these steps, lest they come off as a slick "formula for faith." When human beings approach Almighty God, each does so with his or her own complex uniqueness. Simple pat answers for large and complex questions ought to be viewed with suspicion. Besides, the experiences of one person may not be helpful to another. It may be presumptuous, if not dangerous, for any one of us to lay out formulas for the rest.

Nevertheless, these five specific steps to stronger faith have helped me enormously across the years, and they seem to have helped many who have heard me express them. I have presented this material in more than thirty churches and conferences and shared it with more than two thousand students whom I counseled during my nineteen years as minister of a church near Abilene Christian University. Many of these people have told me they have profited from these suggestions.

I offer them in the hope that you will find them useful as well.

A **Will** to Believe

A first step toward faith...
is to decide whether or not one really wants to believe.

Peter came into our lives over twenty-five years ago when Carolyn and I were living in Salmon Arm, British Columbia. This little village, which spreads picturesquely up the mountainsides from beautiful Shushwap Lake, attracts artists and writers from all over the world. It drew Peter all the way from New Zealand to work as a newspaper reporter while he gathered local color for a novel.

Because Peter was a world traveler with fine intellect and a winsome personality, his invitation list filled quickly. But we were lucky enough to get on it, and that evening with Peter stands among the best of our memories.

As we sat around the cheery fire, Peter entertained us with fascinating stories from faraway places with strange-sounding names. Then, toward the end of the evening, as the fire burned low, Peter grew reflective.

"If you don't mind," he ventured, "I would like to ask you some questions about your religion."

Of course we said yes.

I'll never forget his first question: "Do you really believe there is a God who knows my name?"

Even though my own faith was drowning in doubt at the time, I answered, "Well, yes, that's what we believe." Inside I was thinking, "At least, that is what I want to believe."

Peter continued, "Do you really believe those stories in the Bible are true—that Jesus was born of a virgin and fed a mob with a sardine sandwich? And that after His funeral, He walked out of the cemetery?"

We said, "Well, those things do sound preposterous, especially when you put them that way, but yes, we believe the Bible is true."

Peter grew quiet again for a moment, then observed, "You know, I've lived many places and have met a lot of people. I've noticed, Lynn, that most people are not happy. I have to admit that the few who seem to be happy are mostly folks who believe what you believe."

Then Peter's thunderbolt fell. "I'd give anything in the world if I could believe that...but I just can't do it! I try, but my mind gets in the way!"

"Do you really believe there is a God who knows my name?"

Even now, after all these years, I still feel the enormous helplessness of that moment. I would have given a hundred dollars a word for something appropriate to say. Although I still understand very little about faith, I wish I had known then some things I know now about the dynamics of faith.

My journey has convinced me that doubt is more likely to be rooted in hidden, internal reasons of the will than in conscious, intellectual searching. I do wish I had known that before my conversation with Peter. Peter had probably never come to grips with the real, but hidden, reasons why he found faith impossible. The more I experience the mysteries of the human heart, and the more I listen to the Bible, and the more I struggle with my own faith, the more I am convinced that Peter's faith problem was in his heart, not his head. It wasn't so much that he couldn't believe. Instead, because of his presuppositions, his desires, his relationships, and possibly his emotional history, he really didn't want to believe.

I wish Peter could have known that. I also wish I had told him that the first, and probably the biggest, step toward faith is to honestly decide whether or not you really want to believe.

You can do this, you know. Jesus said that believers can choose to do His father's will. Once you make that decision of your will, although no magic happens, the fog begins to lift. You may still have difficulty understanding your faith and maybe even holding on to it; chances are you will never permanently escape that struggle. But you will be making the first healthy steps on the road to faith when you decide, "Yes, I really want to believe."

A NEED TO BELIEVE

A woman I once knew—a very sharp, accomplished woman, active in local politics—said to me, "Well, Lynn, you know why most Christians believe! They need to. They are emotionally incomplete. Maybe a bad experience in childhood. Insecure. Low self-esteem, or some other psychological need. But for one reason or another, they have this need to believe."

"Do you know what I think about that?" I responded. "I think you are exactly right. If you ask Lynn Anderson why he believes, I will tell you that it is first and foremost because I want to—in fact, because I need to."

If we look inside of ourselves, we may discover something very significant, but something so obvious that it is easily overlooked: There is something in the very nature of a human being that cannot tolerate a vacant heaven. Throughout history, wherever you find human beings, you will also find gods.

Why? My friend may explain it this way: "Basic insecurity; we had to invent the idea of a god because we just couldn't cut it alone." Human psychological need invented God.

But could the reverse be true? Imagine a four-year-old child wandering lost through the aisles of Macy's department store, crying for his mother.

"What's wrong, son?" you ask.

He begs, "I want my mommy."

So you take the little fellow on your lap and say, "Listen, you're a big boy now. The time has come for you to face some facts. Son, you don't *have* a mommy. You're just feeling lonely and insecure. So, to meet your need, you invented this 'mommy' idea in the hopes that you might feel more secure!"

Would the little fellow be convinced?

Of course not! The reason he is crying for his mommy is that he has a mother and has lost touch with her—not vice-versa! And the reason there will be a hole in my reality until I discover a relationship with the Creator of the universe is precisely that *there is a Creator of the universe* and He has designed me for relationship with Him. As surely as male and female long for each other, God and humankind long for each other. Miguel de Unamuno said, "To believe in God is, in the first instance, to wish there may be a God, to be unable to live without Him."[1]

But notice the flip side here, which provides an important clue to why some people have difficulty with faith. Just as *faith* often is deeply rooted in emotional needs to believe, so *unbelief* often has its source in deep, maybe even subliminal, but very real emotional needs *not* to believe.

FAITH BLOCKERS

A college student once lamented to me, "I want to believe, but I just can't."

"Can't? Or won't?" I explored with her. "Is it possible that you have some need to decide that God is not there? For example, could you be afraid of the demands God might make on you? Or do you feel despair because you have tried to behave well enough to meet His standards and you can't? Or are you possibly afraid He will disappoint you—that He will not, or cannot, deliver on His promises?…"

She interrupted, "I guess all of the above, but how did you know?"

Well, I didn't know for sure, but I suspected these possibilities because of my own pilgrimage. I have also listened to a lot of people who felt they could not believe. In my counseling and my conversations, I have heard testimony to all seven of Os Guinness's "doubt roots":

Doubt from failing to remember; from a faulty view of God; because of weak foundations for belief; from the unwillingness to commit oneself; due to a lack of growth; from dominant emotions; from emotional scars which have not been previously healed.[2]

I have also seen, in myself and others, that the true reasons behind our doubts are often hidden from us. Some people live in a form of denial. They say that they really want to believe, while, deep down inside, for a variety of hidden reasons, they really don't want to.

I think this was true of my friend Peter. As I reflect back on my conversation with him, I see a strong possibility that he simply could not expose his *pride* to the ridicule of his peers, who might regard faith as beneath their intellectual dignity. Does this sound familiar? In actual fact, the Bible says we cannot come by much real faith without swallowing our pride. Jesus said, "Blessed are the poor in spirit, for theirs is the kingdom of heaven."[3]

But pride is not the only obstacle that stands in the way of wanting to believe. Faith may also threaten our *vested interests*.

George complained for years that he could not get over the intellectual barriers that stood in the way of full-hearted faith in God. Later George said, "I saw through the rearview mirror that I had latched on to the intellectual barriers because I feared some of my major advertising clients would dump me if they found out I was a believer."

Harry spent several years, in his words, "sorting through the evidences for God, while putting faith on hold," until he finally admitted to himself that deep down he knew God wanted him to close his topless nightclub, and he couldn't imagine himself doing that. "It was my livelihood. Besides, I couldn't quite imagine life without my toys and joys."

Possibly, faith poses a threat to your *career*. My friend Peter, for example, may have felt his career threatened. He was an intellectual and a writer. After all, some intellectuals who have become believers have found themselves shunned in certain literary circles.

Perhaps we may sense that faith could threaten our *relationships*. Peter may have resisted faith because he felt that faith meant walking away from his writing friends, his most fulfilling circle of relationships. (Not, mind you, that he would have actually had to do this, but he might have imagined it would be so.)

My friend Mary felt this social pressure against her faith choice. Mary's husband and his family had begun treating Mary as an outsider when she started visiting a Bible study circle and asking questions about God. Yet she explained her decision against faith in Jesus in terms of intellectual doubts: "It is all too confusing. I find it impossible to decide which world religion to believe."

For Mary, as for many, it was the high cost of following Jesus, not the intellectual obstacles, that made faith difficult. As Jesus said, "If anyone would come after me, he must deny himself and take up his cross and follow me."[4] For some of us, that's just too big of a threat.

HIDDEN ISSUES—SURFACE DOUBTS

Surface rationalization for our doubts may also be rooted in deeper psychological issues. Most of us, for instance, harbor some sort of hidden *fears*. Could a person actually be afraid to believe?

Joe feared the consequences of faith. He reflected, "Sometimes I really hunger for a deeper walk with God, but other times I am afraid of where that leads. I saw faith warp my uncle. He won't pay taxes or go to the doctor because he 'trusts God—not politicians and physicians.' So the year the IRS finally nailed him is the same year my cousin was thrown from a horse and became permanently paralyzed because my uncle wouldn't get medical help. 'God will heal,' he said. Will religion make me a fanatic like my uncle?"

Steven's eyes expressed the same fear as he said, "Why pray to a God who led my dad to quit playing his beautiful violin music and led my sister to smash her TV set and keep her kids out of sports? And I had religion crammed down my throat too. Who needs it?"

Behind some "intellectual" doubt stands the fear that faith may stifle creativity. Joyce, for instance, aspires to be a playwright and to pursue her considerable musical talent as well. "Seems to me," she observed, "that churches are mostly interested in making sure that their people color between the lines. Most Christians I know demand a mindless, deliberate unwillingness to consider alternate viewpoints. They wash all the literary and aesthetic quality out of life. Do I need that?" (By the way, faith didn't seem to wash the creativity out of Michelangelo or J.R.R. Tolkien or Ludwig van Beethoven or C. S. Lewis or Leonardo da Vinci or Amy Grant or Fanny Crosby or Michael W. Smith or…!)

> Could a person actually be afraid to believe?

A number of people have confided that they hold faith at an impersonal distance for fear of closing their options. This particular fear seems very "in" right now. In the 1950s and 60s, the big faith blocker was science. But nowadays, the big issue seems to be maintaining the freedom to choose. People are skittish about long-term commitments. They assume they will make several career changes over a lifetime. Many postpone marriage, stating they are "not ready for a commitment." As one young woman, a medical student, told me, "If I lock in to a mate now, I miss a lot." It's no wonder that faith often gets deferred to keep the options open.

For others, doubt may be rooted in feelings of anger. Perhaps they feel victimized by God, identifying the God of traditional Christianity with racial prejudice, sexism, social injustice, and religious bigotry. (Paradoxically, they are thus approving the values rooted in biblical teaching: justice, love, and mercy.)

For some, the anger may be more personal. During college, Lonny was the guy most of us envied. His faith glowed, and people gravitated to his winsome personality. Ten years later, Lonny, now a successful stockbroker, told me he couldn't bring himself to come close to God. "If there is a God at all, He sure has a strange sense of humor. Lynn, I'm gay. I didn't make myself this way. I'll never have a family, never feel normal, and never experience love—at least not with your God's approval. I'm not denying He is there; I just don't think I want to have anything to do with Him!"

SCARRED FAITH: THE FAMILY FACTOR

Likely, the most powerful psychological faith blockers are deep scars hidden beneath the waterline of consciousness. A number of these buried issues clutter the pathway to faith. For example, research by David Lewis, Carley Dodd, and Darryl Tippens isolates major family factors that bear a direct impact upon faith. They found that:

> Through the experience of parental security, trust and loyalty, the child develops the willingness to be bound to God. We are not saying that children lacking these spiritual nutrients are doomed to reject God, but their route to God is often sadly troubled and difficult.[5]

Possibly this family factor explains Bonnie's doubts. Bonnie made several appointments then broke them before the day she first plodded into my study angry, depressed, and—in her own words— "agnostic." Bonnie is unusually intelligent, and she had done a lot of thinking and reading before announcing, "It has become intellectually impossible for me to really believe any longer. If God exists at all, He must be an egomaniac. Why else would He demand that everyone bow down and worship Him. How can I trust someone like that?"

Bonnie and I went through months of intricate "intellectual" dialogue without getting anywhere. Then one day the real source of Bonnie's doubts finally tumbled out. That day Bonnie stormed through my door, slamming it behind her. Two babies were with the sitter, and now Bonnie was pregnant again. Not only had her alcoholic husband lost his job, he had terrorized the family all night with a knife, smiling grotesquely and cooing that it was better for them all to "go home to Jesus."

Somehow that night of trauma brought to light a long history of physical and emotional abuse that Bonnie had successfully "forgotten." Her mother had periodically whipped Bonnie while praying and reading Scripture verses to her. Her father, a church deacon, had habitually intimidated her into lying to cover for his sexual indiscretions. And then she had married Toby, whose equally dysfunctional but also fanatically religious family had eventually driven him to drink. No wonder Bonnie was mad at God! But until Toby hit the bottle, she had managed to readjust her childhood memories enough that she had no conscious memory of abuse. She wasn't even aware of the hidden roots of her anger.

Don carried similar scars that got in the way of his faith. Don's mother had never missed church. She had carried her Bible in her purse. She even quoted Scripture to the postman and boasted to her friends that Donnie would one day be a minister. And Don had tried seminary but concluded that he didn't believe much anymore. In his mind, "light from his graduate studies" had enlightened him to the point that faith was now impossible.

When Don's mother died, Don discovered that she had cut him out of her will. In his rage Don was finally able to get in touch with the fact that his mother had sexually molested him for years, beginning before his earliest memories. It was not really God whom Don could not believe in, but the warped image of God instilled in him by his mother.

As Lewis, Dodd, and Tippens observe, long-ago family issues can easily tip the scale on whether a person truly wants to have faith or, deep down, wants nothing to do with God:

> When children learn to feel safe and know they will not be betrayed, then they are more likely to blossom as adolescents capable of a true personal relationship with God.... [But] children deprived of a sense of security and significance, especially in early life, may remain emotionally dwarfed; sometimes they

simply may be unable to commit themselves to others—whether God or humans.[6]

Since churches in some ways resemble extended families, the scars of bad church experiences can also subconsciously hinder faith. When people feel betrayed by someone who, to them, represents God, they quite naturally retaliate with disbelief.

Mark, for instance, really wonders about God. His contact with faith comes primarily through his ex-wife and her family—and very little in that experience has inclined him toward believing. Their marriage began badly and went downhill from there. Sue was critical and silent and recoiled from sex. Mark found consolation in a woman friend, whom he ended up going to bed with—once. Mark makes no excuse for his behavior. In fact, he was so remorseful that he immediately confessed to Sue, who, without counseling or even further conversation, promptly filed for divorce. Neither she nor her family ever spoke to Mark again, despite his repeated attempts at reconciliation. Sue's father is a church officer, and Sue is a Sunday-school teacher. Mark knows that Sue's father has cut ethical corners in business. Mark says, "I don't blame God, because I'm not sure I believe in God anymore."

> Bad ideas can be as damaging as bad people.

Mark, Don, and Bonnie are only representatives of the large crowds of doubters who have been scarred through betrayal by professing believers—relatives, ministers, elders, business partners, mates, mentors, or media evangelists. Anger, disillusionment, and mistrust over this kind of betrayal easily become transferred to God. And, again, the transfer sometimes occurs at hidden, subconscious levels that may surface in the disguise of doubt.

THEOLOGICAL TRAPS

Bad ideas can be as damaging as bad people—and these, too, can be part of our legacy from the past. One pervasive theological trap is the belief that God is the source of all suffering, disaster, and sadness.

If we think this way, we naturally blame God for any bad thing that befalls us. "If there is a loving God," we reason, "why did He bring this on me? Or if He is so powerful, why would He allow it?"

Then there are the "guilters and stressors." Many people are driven away from faith by faulty ideas about God's nature and His expectations.

At one season of my own faith life, I felt that the closer I got to God, the more He hurt me. I was haunted by a searing sense of never being good enough, never measuring up. Others have felt this too! During those dark days, God was a condemning judge who demanded the impossible from me. He offered me no hope, unless I knew exactly what was right and did it perfectly. And even though I publicly would say, "God is love," privately, inside of me, there was no meaning in the phrase. Nothing about God seemed attractive to me.

I began to feel like William C. Kerley did when he wrote:

> The sports fans in this ball game are beginning to yell with more regularity and louder, "We wuz robbed! Somebody has reneged on the promises!"
>
> *"I am come that you might have life and have it to the full."*
>
> And here we are so burdened.
>
> *"He who drinks of this water will never thirst."*
>
> And we with parched throats go from one dry well to another seeking relief.
>
> *"Come unto me all of you who are weary and over-burdened and I will give you rest."*
>
> Yet, what we are given is another job, put on another committee, given some more rules and obligations, always confronted with doing more, being other—and always on the go, always on the go.[7]

Of course, it was not really God who hurt me, but *bad ideas about God.* I had soaked up part of the gospel without internalizing the whole, balanced heart of it. This erroneous view left me with no hope; I was living with condemnation without forgiveness, judgment without mercy, guilt without grace. No wonder I had trouble wanting to believe!

HIDDEN IN THE HEART

The parade of possible hidden faith blockers goes on. This book could not describe them all, even if I knew what they were, which I don't. Possibly you identify with some of the examples listed here. You could likely add your own to the list.

The fact is most of us carry some of this baggage, but we may so cleverly disguise our hidden resistance to faith that we even fool ourselves and on the surface identify the source of our doubts as "intellectual problems" that "make it difficult to believe."

This tendency to confuse the sources of our unbelief may be further complicated by common cultural attitudes about faith and intellect. The popular perception nowadays implies that choosing faith demands either ignorance or intellectual dishonesty, that scientific, historical, and psychological "facts" will not allow us to believe in the God of the Bible and still maintain our intellectual integrity; thus, faith would be intellectual suicide for educated people. This perception is propagated by the media and other influential sources—not as overt or blatant ridicule, but in the form of subtle assertions and assumptions.

Curiously, Nathan Glazer in the *New Republic* argues the exact opposite—that the thing wrong with believing is that only intellectually slick people can do the mental gymnastics essential to faith:

I myself believe the terrible wounds suffered by religion in the past three hundred years, primarily because of the spread of the scientific worldview throughout society, cannot be healed. Religion, which was once a belief for the everybody, and a matter of policy for the elite, has changed its character. Today faith is only possible for the sophisticated, who can explain—or explain away—the implications of modern science and scientific thinking. The majority, regardless of what they say on public-opinion polls, can no longer be deeply affected by religious faith. For them, henceforth, religion will be a matter of social utility.[8]

On the one hand, can faith not withstand intelligent examination? On the other, does faith demand intellectual superiority? Neither view can be substantiated.

The truth is that great minds fall on both sides of faith. So do ignorant ones. But all this is really beside the point, because a fair and loving God knows that anyone can choose to believe. Faith is not the privileged domain either of the ignorant or of a select few who make up the intellectual elite. The heart is the root problem, not the head. We can choose to become believers or we can choose to be unbelievers. Either way, our *hearts* are making a choice, whether we realize it or not.

And that simple fact brings us to another important source of unbelief. Quite simply: A *person may not be able to have faith because he or she simply doesn't want to do things God's way.* Often the reason we don't want to believe is that we don't want God messing around in our playhouses. In biblical language, we don't want to repent or turn around. So at some deep level, we choose not to believe.

Often our faith is sapped by hidden sin. Burton Coffman, a veteran minister, pointed this out to me a decade ago in a very earthy way. He heard me preach a sermon in which I suggested that faith is at its taproot a decision of the will. After the sermon, Burton beelined to me and boomed, "Decision of the will. That's right, boy. It's also a moral decision."

I asked him to help me understand more of what he meant.

"Well," he explained, "we have a way of adjusting our theology to fit our ethics. For example, you show me a preacher who is getting too sophisticated and broad-minded for the gospel, and I'll show you a preacher who is shacked up with his secretary!"

Now, Burton didn't mean that every broad-minded preacher has some hanky-panky going on the side! But he understood very well how hidden sin—sin which is not dealt with—buckles the knees of faith. All varieties of hidden sin have that effect, not just the scarlet sin in Coffman's colorful quote.

FACING THE REAL ISSUE

For some time I taught annual seminars on self-esteem, goal setting, and positive thinking to a business group. One evening toward the end of the class, I pushed aside the supplied textbook and ad-libbed, "Now fellows, this stuff may up your sales or lift you over a few blue Mondays. But if I were to advise you to put your life down on it, I'd be as phony as an undertaker trying to look sad at a twenty-thousand-dollar funeral! You've got to build your life on something solid! I sure do. My self-esteem comes from knowing that I matter to God. My goals are shaped by my understanding of God's purposes. I can maintain a positive outlook because I believe my future is in the hands of a loving and almighty God."

At this point, Tom interrupted me. Tom was a powerfully built, athletic, and handsome ex-Marine officer. He wore a natty suit and drove exotic wheels. Everyone in the room envied his booming business and his powerful presence.

Tom charged, "You don't have to drag religion into this!"

I definitely felt intimidated. But I nervously explained, "You know where I am coming from. Surely you didn't expect me to teach three classes on basic values and never mention God! Frankly, I don't know anywhere else I'd turn to find real values."

After class, as I headed across the parking lot through the rain, I heard footsteps sloshing behind me. I turned to see Tom approaching at a brisk trot. I thought, *Uh-oh. I'm about to be treated to a Marine knuckle sandwich.*

But to my surprise Tom wilted like a child and begged, "Lynn, you've got to help me. I'm a frightened little boy in a man's body. The last time I felt alive was when I was killing 'gooks' in Vietnam! I don't like my value system. I don't feel good about cheating on my wife several times in the last few weeks. I spend more time drinking and chasing women than I do working, yet I still have more money than I can spend. I am bored to death. You've got to help me, but…don't lay any of that God rap on me, because I can't believe in that stuff!"

We headed for an all-night restaurant, where for nearly two hours Tom's life story tumbled out. The longer Tom talked, the more obvious his problem seemed to me. I tried to steer the conversation gently, but in my emotion (and likely my nervousness), my words came out more bluntly than I had intended. "Listen, Tom. I don't think your problem is that you are too smart to believe. I think it is that you are too wicked!"

Tom looked shocked: "Say what, now?"

So I blundered on. "You don't want God messing around in your playhouse. If you sold out to God, you would have to give up a lot of playthings and security blankets. You might lose your image, too, and you simply can't face that. Besides, bad treatment at the hands of your hypocritical granddad gave you a pretty negative view of God to start with. Right?"

Tom looked away for a long moment, then reflected, "You know, Lynn, no one has ever said anything like that to me before. I guess I find myself thinking you may be right. But what you call my 'wickedness' is my way of dealing with things. This stuff I am hanging on to is my painkiller; at least it gets me through the night and props up my self-esteem. If I drop all this stuff and take the leap toward God, what happens if He is not there—or if He turns out to be like my grandpa? Then I would have lost everything!"

> My self-esteem comes from knowing that I matter to God.

"Tom, my friend," I couldn't help but say, "seems to me you have just put your finger on the real issue."

It would be nice to say that Tom trusted Christ there in that restaurant. He didn't—and the last time I saw him before losing track of him, he was still struggling. But as he gradually came in touch with the real impediments to faith, he began reconsidering his decision. He was beginning to believe again, he thought. At least now he was facing the real issue. Tom finally realized that if he was an unbeliever, it was because he wanted it that way!

Helmut Thielicke, in *How to Believe Again*, comments:

> If a person learns to bring God into the picture and therefore begins to believe, then he ceases to be so passionately self-willed. Looking back, he discovers that it was this very autonomy, this centering his life on his own ego, that made him seek unbelief and made him fear that faith would threaten his self-will. This and nothing else creates my real inhibition about dealing with the question of God's existence. For it is precisely my self-will that I must put on the line when I wager on God.[9]

Deciding What You Want

Our friends Peter and Tom and the rest of the crowd in this chapter illustrate what Jesus said clearly—that making the choice to go with God is the first step toward faith: "If anyone chooses to do God's will, he will find out whether my teaching comes from God or whether I speak on my own."[10]

Let me reiterate that: The very first and most important step toward faith is to decide whether or not you really want to believe and honestly to face the reasons why you choose what you choose.

If you struggle with doubt but think you want faith, first make an effort to be brutally honest with yourself. Take inventory of your inner self. Could there be any reason—either conscious or buried in your subconscious—why you might not want to believe? If you think your answer is yes, good. You are moving toward an honest decision about whether or not you really want to believe.

You may ask, "But how do I take such an 'internal inventory'?"

You can begin privately by *journaling* your behavior and feelings over a period of weeks, even months. Periodically reread your journal to spot telltale signals or recurring cycles.

Also, when you feel ready for it, *objective friends* can help. You might ask a trusted friend to read the journal and ask his or her diagnosis.

Any of a number of helpful books can help you sort out the underlying issues that may be holding you back from full-hearted faith. Hugh Missildine's classic book *Your Inner Child of the Past* contains information and exercises that have enabled me and thousands of others to put a finger on the real hidden feelings. Equally helpful are M. Scott Peck's groundbreaking books *The Road Less Traveled* and *People of the Lie*. To help you handle negative feelings about God stemming from past religious or family experience, let me suggest *Toxic Faith*, by Stephen Arterburn and Jack Felton; Arterburn's *The Angry Man*; *Inside Out*, by Larry Crabb; *The Blessing*, by Gary Smalley and John Trent; *The Subtle Power of Spiritual Abuse*, by David Johnson and Jeff VanVonderen; and *Tired of Trying to Measure Up*, by Jeff VanVonderen.[11]

When you begin to feel even braver, a *group experience* can help. One of the most revealing experiences I have personally walked through was a semester spent in a group-dynamics class where we all became vulnerable to each other and sometimes brutally honest. Various support groups, prayer circles, Bible study groups, and accountability groups can serve a similar function.

Personally, I have found that consulting a well-trained *psychologist or pastoral counselor* can be a very useful aid to self-understanding. Occasional cycles of such counseling can be helpful for anyone, especially those troubled by strongly ambivalent feelings about God and faith. In my own experience, some parts of my emotional history that fed my doubt were buried so deeply and disguised so well that I would never have recognized them without the skillful help of a trained professional.

Even if you discover that you honestly don't want to believe, at least this process of uncovering your real motives will enable you to deal with your decision more openly and honestly. And if you spot some hidden faith blocker, processing that "glitch" in your nature or history will probably move you toward healthier living, whether or not this clears the pathway to faith.

A DAILY DECISION

Of course, I assume that if you are reading this book, most likely you have long since decided that you do want to believe. You may need to keep on deciding tomorrow morning and every morning after that. And you will need to continue being honest about your doubts and their roots.

Faith can't be stockpiled like flour and sugar and canned goods. We can make some lifestyle decisions that may bolster our faith in hard times—like studying Scripture and building relationships with people who believe. But those preparations cannot exempt us from the need to keep on choosing, to keep on making the decision to believe.

I made that will/choice decision again this morning when I rolled out of bed. The only faith I have today is as fresh and new as this morning's sunrise.

But I am still believing! Are you still believing? I plan to make that decision again tomorrow morning. I hope you want to as well, because only you can decide for you!

And then what?

Touching Faith

A second step toward faith…
is to go where faith is being nourished.

If you decided to grow orchids, you probably would not move to the North Pole. If you want to study free enterprise, you would not likely enroll in the University of Beijing. And if you want your faith to flourish, it only makes sense to go where faith is. So the second step toward stronger faith is to seek out healthy believers and to steer clear of environments that erode your faith.

This, of course, is not to suggest that believers should hide in Christian ghettos. But your faith will not grow if you spend all your time and energy absorbing the value systems of people who don't believe!

Instead, pull alongside a few authentic, informed, infectious believers. Pick their brains, observe their lifestyle, study what makes them tick. In fact, begin now to create a whole new circle of "significant others" who practice the kind of faith you long for.

A SIGNIFICANT CIRCLE

Karen is a minister's wife, but she still needs her circle of spiritually significant others to nurture her faith. Through them, she has touched faith and experienced growth. Maybe it's because Karen doesn't have sisters and her mother lives halfway across the nation. But in every church that she and her husband have served (six so far), Karen has taken the initiative to search out an older, mature Christian woman to be a special encourager. Karen and her encourager spend time together. They pray together, they have breakfast together, they laugh and cry together. These special friendships have brought growth and faith development to Karen. Our faith grows when we go where faith is!

> When I am at loose ends, temptations seem to loom larger and my faith tends to fade back.

Long ago I discovered my own need for a circle of faith nourishers to whom I could go for healing. At times I feel as much like a doubter as a believer, so I have to feed on the faith of others who are blessed with the gift of strong faith. I also need help to keep on doing what is right! Doing right can mean anything from maintaining spiritual disciplines to resisting moral temptation. I depend heavily on the accountability of a group to keep my faith on track. Frankly, I believe we all need such accountability.

Arterburn and Felton's observation matches my own experience when they point out that usually "a person cannot just read a good book and have a radical life change (that is, without divine intervention). The group provides accountability and a new bond to replace the old one."[1]

The Bible also underscores this observation; the apostle James writes, "Confess your sins to each other and pray for each other so that you may be healed."[2]

The men and women with whom I fellowshipped for years as fellow church staff members knew one another well enough that we could pick up on the telltale flicker of an eyelash, and we came to trust one another enough to raise the probing questions. I could never have survived without the love and support of those beloved staff colleagues and several other confidants and friends elsewhere.

When I moved from Abilene, Texas, to Dallas to isolate myself for eighteen months of writing, I felt naked and vulnerable out on my own, with no one to encourage me and no one to answer to. So I gathered around me two circles of accountability—one a band of fellow ministers, the other a small circle of believing businessmen. These significant circles kept me afloat during those lonely times when my faith could easily have faltered.

For years, when traveling alone, I have planned ahead to check in with specific Christian friends upon hitting the permissive disconnectedness of whatever distant city. I need both accountability and encouragement. When I am at loose ends, temptations seem to loom larger and my faith tends to fade back. So I don't trust myself. I'm not sure I have enough faith to carry on in isolation. In fact, I'm not sure human beings are built to do that!

MAINTAINING FAITH CONNECTIONS

You, too, may need to build encouragement and accountability into your life by establishing connections with a study circle or a prayer group or by plugging into Christian social circles, recreational groups, or task forces that network you with robust believers.

The traditional Sunday church services and classes are helpful, but many folks find that Sunday's input isn't enough to sustain them through the week. Midweek classes may only add more pressure points to an already unbearable schedule. In addition, some of these events wind up asking for more *activity*, not offering more personal spiritual development.

If you want to keep moving along the faith road, you simply must carve out time to be with supportive, vibrantly believing people—and not just for religious activities. Going where faith is means taking your *whole life* (including your social life) where faithful people are. Making new friends and going new places with them—to the gym, to the golf course, to drama clubs, to community-college classes, and to coffee shops—are vital parts of a comprehensive faith nourishment strategy.

In fact, there are several other excellent ways for busy people to go where faith is. For example…

- One group of young mothers meets in a van during their kids' practice times at the soccer field. They grab this downtime for mutual faith building, alternating daily between Bible study and prayer sessions. (On game days, of course, they become their children's loudest cheerleaders!)
- A scattered group of traveling businessmen and women has mutually agreed to a program of individual disciplines. Each reads Scripture, reflects, and keeps a daily spiritual journal. The group meets periodically for a discussion and prayer breakfast. But most of the time they connect once a week by conference call. From all over the nation they gather over the phone lines for thirty minutes of conversation, prayer, and accountability. (They rotate the cost of the call among the group members.)
- Four high-powered Texas business and professional men commit to read through a designated short book of the Bible each week. Then they meet at five o'clock on Saturday mornings, before racquetball, to discuss practical "so whats."
- Bernice hosts a "brown bag" Bible study and prayer circle on Tuesdays at her office for women who work in the downtown area. Cory hosts a similar gathering at a nearby restaurant for the interested men and women in his brokerage firm. The members of both groups report that they feel spiritually rootless and resourceless without their time together.
- Will, a Dallas businessman, distributes lists of selected tapes, articles, and books to a group of friends. These men and women work through the materials individually and maintain periodic written and telephone contact. Then once each year Will and his wife, Fran, host a three-day retreat

for those friends who have studied a year's common resources.

- A group of graduate students retreat monthly to practice some solitude and silence and to keep their priorities focused. Recently, for example, they met for a Saturday breakfast, watched Woody Allen's movie *Crimes and Misdemeanors*, then spent half the day reflecting on the faith questions it raises.

THE RIGHT CHURCH

Wherever else you go to connect with people of faith, make sure you dive into the life of a good church.

You may protest, "Hold on a minute. My experience with church is one of the main obstacles to my faith." You might even object, "You wouldn't believe the garbage that goes on in my church!"

But I do know. After thirty years of ministry in small churches and large, at the center of denominational politics, and having counseled with hundreds of church folk—believe me, I know! I might even be able to tell you a few things you haven't heard!

Of course churches have great limitations, even liabilities. They are, after all, collections of human beings! Churches are not meant to be perfect; a church is meant to be a place where we messed up and doubting people gather in various kinds of circles and look into one another's faces to help one another keep on believing. Churches are not meant to be trophy cases for spiritual superstars but more like emergency wards staffed by the walking wounded.

When you finish writing your list of complaints, look around you for the people whose faith you most admire. The overwhelming majority of them are active in churches, and their faith is being nourished there in spite of all the church's shortcomings.

If you are not currently involved in a church, start looking. But just walking in the front door of a church full of strangers probably isn't the best way to start. Instead, take your time and be careful and methodical. And if you feel a little timid, ask for help.

You might not even know where to begin. For starters, look for a friend you like and respect who is a churchgoer and ask about his or her church. If it sounds interesting and authentic, ask if you can visit church with him or her and meet some of your friend's other friends—maybe in a small group at first. Try a church softball team, a singles group, a Sunday class, or some other small group. These small group encounters will give you a feel for what that church is like "behind the public relations."

When you hear a minister whose message and person connects with you, give him or her a call. Ask for an appointment or, better yet, invite the minister to lunch. Explain your feelings and doubts to the minister. Most ministers will be helpful to you in connecting with a good church and, more specifically, with the exact group within the church that will be most helpful to your growth in faith.

Eugene C. Roehlkepartain's research on what makes faith mature pinpoints some qualities you might look for, especially in a large church:

1. The congregation has an effective formal Christian education program, including Sunday school classes, Bible studies, adult forums, family events, music and drama programs, and new-member classes.
2. Members perceive that their congregation encourages questions, challenges thinking, and expects learning.
3. The congregation successfully recruits members to volunteer to help people in need.
4. Members perceive that their Sunday worship is of high quality.
5. Members see their congregation as warm and friendly.
6. Members personally experience other members' care and concern.[3]

If you are already in a church but not finding the encouragement and accountability you need, look again. Seek out small groups where you can plug into the full life of faith. Pray for guidance in locating a place of service that can also give you a chance to rub shoulders with persons of faith. Ask your minister or another staff person for suggestions.

Sometimes, but only as a last resort, it may be necessary to change churches. I don't mean "church hop"—going from congregation to congregation and leaving when you don't get your way. There is no such thing as a perfect church. But if after much prayer and hard work you find that your faith cannot grow in your particular faith environment, go elsewhere. Being involved in the Body of Christ is just too vital to your faith for you to risk doing without it.

GO WHERE BELIEVERS ARE

Keep in mind throughout your search that faith is neither to be discovered nor to be lived out in solitude, but is initiated, refined, and strengthened in a community of faith. My heart resonates with John Westerhoff, who wrote:

Faith cannot be taught by any method of instruction; we can only teach religion. We can know about religion, but we can only expand in faith, act in faith, live in faith. Faith can be inspired within a community of faith, but it cannot be given to one person by another. Faith is expressed, transformed, and made meaningful by persons sharing their faith in an historical, tradition-bearing community of faith.[4]

The community of faith is where our particular way of looking at life is expressed, fostered, and given meaning. We need one another. In spite of the weaknesses of the church, if you want faith, go where the believers are.

> In spite of the weaknesses of the church, if you want faith, go where the believers are.

Take it from the Browns. They had not been to church in a long time. A friend came by to visit, and as they sat around the fireplace, the friend listened to their story. The Browns said they didn't need church. They felt their faith dwindling and decided that the church wasn't helping them any. They didn't feel the need for fellowship with any kind of Christian small group either.

"We felt like we had more chance at faith in God if we just kind of went it on our own," explained Gerald Brown. "Why, I seem to feel more worshipful out on the lake fishing at dawn or walking the back fairway than I ever did at church!"

After listening for an hour or two, the friend finally broke his silence. "I want you to watch very carefully what I'm going to do."

He walked over to the fireplace, picked up the poker, and reached into the bed of the glowing coals. He pulled one single large and bright coal out of the center of the heat and slid it to the corner of the hearth by itself. Within a few moments, the coal began to lose its glow, turned gray, sent up a wisp of smoke, then turned black. Then the friend raised the poker again and shoved the dead coal back into the fire. In a few moments, the coal had lost its dull blackness and recaptured its radiant glow.

They all sat still awhile. Then Brown cleared his throat and acknowledged, "Yes, I guess you could say our faith has lost its glow. Faith doesn't do too well in solitary, does it?"

How true, Brown, how true. If we really want to grow, we must choose to go where faith is.

The vertical reason Christians come together is to offer worship to God. The horizontal reason Christians come together is to encourage one another to keep making the faith decision. Faith will usually falter unless Christians find a regular time and place where they can look into one another's faces and say, in one way or another, with honesty and with no fancy God-talk, "I am still believing. Are you still believing? Help me overcome my unbelief." We really do need to keep saying this to one another.

So once you have decided that you really want to believe, go where faith is. Faith-building relationships are essential for growth. And it is essential that faith—newfound or renewed—rests upon a trustworthy object.

Targeting Faith

9

A *third* step toward faith…
is to clarify the object of one's faith.

Those of us reared in Western Canada are experts on one thing: ice! (We have it down cold.)

Let me explain the basic truth about ice. Ice comes in two kinds: thick ice and thin ice! Thick ice you can walk on. Thin ice you stay clear of.

When my Tennessee wife first moved to Canada, she didn't trust any ice much—not even thick ice. After the first heavy fall freeze, we took the family for a "walk-n-slide" on the glassy surface of Woods Lake. But Carolyn was nervous about the whole expedition.

Expanding lake ice often groans and cracks even when it is thick enough to support a tank. That sound was new to Carolyn, however, and it scared the daylights out of her. She imagined the whole family falling through the ice and drowning. But then an air-plane broke over the ridge, droned in a wide circle, and—lo and behold—landed on the shiny surface of the lake. As if that wasn't enough to prove the ice trustworthy, next a truck drove out on the ice to meet the plane.

After that, Carolyn calmed down and began to trust the ice a little. Not very much. But then, you don't need much faith for thick ice to support you. On the other hand, you can place all the faith in the world on thin ice and drown by faith!

This is the basic truth about faith too. The most important issue is not the amount of faith we can muster but the trustworthiness of the object of our faith. As Arterburn and Felton say,

> God does not need a lot of faith. He needs only a little seed of healthy faith to work with. Christ described this small faith as being the size of a mustard seed (Matthew 17:20). From that small speck of faith the impossible can be accomplished *as long as the focus is on God.*[1]

So *be careful about the object of your faith.* Make sure you trust something that can support you.

TRUSTING THE UNTRUSTWORTHY

No matter how intense and sincere your faith, if it is based in anything less than God through Jesus Christ, it is idolatry, and idols will always let you down. More important, idolatry will derail your trust in God.

Idols take many forms. As Dan Anders wrote,

> We all trust some ultimate reality:
>> the thought-world of the idealist
>> the pleasure world of the hedonist
>> the static world of the determinist
>> the practical world of the pragmatist
>> the irrational world of the existentialist
>> the secular world of the humanist
>> the theocratic world of the theist.
>
> The point is that there are no unbelievers. All of us believe in something that is our "realest real"—what Paul Tillich called our "Ultimate Concern."[2]

Some of us, however, have tried to believe in objects not worth our trust. Some of these trusts are downright dangerous.

For example, a few years back, hundreds of people moved to Oregon to believe in a strange little fellow called the Bagwan Maharishi, who drove up and down the road in a Rolls Royce. He took the money and ran! More recently, millions of Iraqis placed their faith in Saddam Hussein, with even far more disastrous results.

Misplacing trust can be spiritually perilous as well. If I put my faith in a minister, chances are he will let me down. Thousands of sincere people have been bilked by a handful of TV evangelists who ignored the law, squandered millions, and collapsed morally. Others put their faith in Jim Jones, who led them to their deaths in Guyana. Of course, not every minister is like a Media Gantry or a Jim Jones. Most ministers are authentic. But even the most sincere minister is a human being and sooner or later will reveal feet of clay.

> Faith in faith is little more than a form of self-hypnosis.

We have already recommended that a growing faith should be nurtured in a good church. But if I place all my trust in a church, it, too, will sooner or later disappoint me. Churches cannot save us. They are not perfect. Mistakes, mixed motives, and wrong attitudes mar some of the best efforts of the most compassionate churches.

Some people even trust in faith itself. But faith in faith is little more than a form of self-hypnosis. Years back, some radio networks carried spots entitled "This I Believe." Assorted celebrities attempted to lift the nation's spirit through short, positive sound-bytes about things they "truly believed."

However, little substance could be found in *what* was being believed. As a friend of mine wryly commented, "The bytes pitched approximately 75 percent 'I,' 20 percent 'believe,' and only about 5 percent 'this.'" In essence, they were simply urging the country to believe in believism.

Some faith-in-faith distortions may even look relatively harmless. One frosty fall evening, back during the nineteen fun years that I chaplained a college football team, I saw faith in faith at work on the sidelines. We led by two points with time running out, but then our opponents pounced on our fumble at our five-yard line. A huge linebacker grabbed his helmet to head out onto the field. But first he fell at my feet on his knees in the mud and pleaded, "Pray with me, chaplain." Then he began to chant, "I can do all things through Christ who strengthens me!" I couldn't help glancing across the field to see if the opposing fullback was kneeling too!

Humorous? Yes. Harmless? Maybe not. The linebacker appeared to have more faith in his own faith than in God. Besides, God is not honored by attempts to manipulate Him to our own ends.

For some religious people the object of faith may be faith in the right answers. ("Okay, maybe I display no spiritual fruit, and maybe I am the hardest guy in town to get along with, but, boy, can I quote you stacks of Bible verses.") This pugnacious brand of "faith" can hardly be expected to bring satisfaction or peace with God!

It's possible to displace faith in God with faith in the Bible as my God—or, should I say, in one's particular view of what Scripture is and interpretation of what it says. While I believe the Bible is the Word of God, it is *not* God! We do not worship the Book of God but the God of the Book.

Possibly the most subtle idolatry enthusiastically worships distortions of the true God. Yes! It is possible to trust wrong notions of the right God to the detriment of our own social, psychological, and spiritual welfare.

For example, some see a loving God as a sentimental and benign old grandfather in the sky who lavishly dishes out health and wealth, who can be counted on to spoil His children with nothing but prosperity, peace, success, and pleasure. This god looks attractive up front. But he fosters self-centeredness. And in the end, he produces disillusioned followers whose "faith" hasn't "paid off" in ways they expected. When people place faith in an erroneous view of God, it has serious repercussions!

Other people see God as a judgmental tyrant who drives His subjects by guilt and fear. Since we tend to become like the gods we worship, this god produces neurotic personalities and narrow-minded churches.

Some try to believe in a God who accepts only those who can be good enough. Those of us who have tried to believe in that god soon lost hope. This god drove me to nightmares in my early twenties. During that time, I repeatedly dreamed the same Freudian dream several times per year. At least I think it was Freudian! Or was it a dream?

Night after night, I found myself in a swimming pool full of water, the surface of which was covered with inflated balloons. Somehow it was my responsibility to submerge all the balloons at once. I gathered them, sat on them, lay on them, anything to get them under. But they kept popping back up. If I tucked them under my right side, they burbled up on the left. As the dream ended, I could see something written on each balloon—the names of my pet sins! Then I woke up in a cold sweat.

No professional analyst is needed to understand the psychological roots of these dreams. I believe these dreams were symptoms of bad theology. I was trying to be good enough to be accepted by God, to defeat my sins on my own. But I was fighting a losing battle. Such a distorted view of God can make doubters feel like giving up.

The One Dependable Object of Trust

Oh, yes! False objects of faith inevitably bring disillusionment and sometimes cause deep and lasting damage. One must be discriminating about what one believes. Healthy faith cannot be built on "the caricatures of God, created by our self-obsessed society." It cannot be based on what we want God to be or what we want God to do. Healthy faith grows when idols "are replaced with the real God of the Bible."[3]

Not even knowledge about God is the dependable object of trust. He alone is.

A college student related the moment this realization first broke through to him. He was a good churchgoer. He knew what to do and when. Stand. Sit. Bow the head. Drop in money. Everything at the right time. But God never seemed personal to him till that one ordinary Sunday as the congregation bowed their heads for the benediction. Reality hit him like a bolt of lightning: "Hey, we're talking to God!"

In his excitement, he forgot himself and grabbed the guy next to him before the public benediction ended and shouted so loud his voice rang through the whole sanctuary, "Hey, man, you know what we're doing? We're talking to *God!* We're *actually* talking to *God!*"

Eyes popped open and bowed heads swiveled curiously. But for this young man it was a magnificent moment of insight!

If I earned a million dollars an hour for the rest of my days, I couldn't pay for the meaning that has come into my life since the reality first dawned on me that God is listening to me and God loves me—Lynn Anderson. In spite of my sins, He loves me! And He said it from a cross!

In the Common on the campus of the University of Victoria in Canada hung this poster:

> *Question:* What do these four people have in common?
> Abraham Lincoln
> Martin Luther King
> Florence Nightingale
> Blaise Pascal
> *Answer:* They all had the same teacher. As did most of the people who have made the big positive difference. His name was Jesus Christ! You may want to reconsider Him as an option for a world in decline. He has proved to be a worthy object of faith.

The poster is right on target. The bull's-eye of all worthwhile faith is painted by John the apostle: "Believe that *Jesus is the Christ, the Son of God,* and…by believing you may have life in his name."[4]

THE CASE FOR TRUSTING JESUS

One day I struck up a conversation with a retiree sitting on a park bench. Somehow we got around to talking about Jesus, and I asked him, "Who do you think Jesus is?"

He reflected a bit then smiled with what seemed a hint of condescension as he replied, "To me, Jesus is a nice idea that nobody takes very seriously—sort of like Santa Claus."

Does Jesus sometimes feel like this to you? And what real evidence supports the contrary?

Pretend that we are in a court of law. The historical reality of Jesus is on trial. Testimony begins with a group of witnesses from secular history.

First, an ancient Roman emperor, Trajan, is called to the witness stand. He admits to launching severe persecution against the early Christians. He also testifies that Pliny, the governor of a minor Roman province called Bithynia, wrote him about these proceedings. Pliny had heard rumors that something was to be done to the Christians, but he wasn't sure what. The exchange of letters between Pliny and Trajan discussed the treatment of the "followers of that Galilean."[5] Neither Trajan nor Pliny called Jesus "God," but they both affirmed that He was real.

Next witness is Tacitus, a Roman historian and a contemporary of Jesus. He declares that Jesus was put to death "under the reign of Tiberius Caesar."[6] This corroborates testimony of the Bible that Jesus was baptized "in the fifteenth year of the reign of Tiberius Caesar."[7]

We call a third witness to the stand, a Jewish historian about thirty years younger than Jesus named Flavius Josephus. He says,

> Now there was about this time Jesus, a wise man…if it be lawful to call him a man. For he was a doer of wonderful works, a teacher of such men as receive truth with pleasure. He drew over to him both many of the Jews and many of the Gentiles.[8]

So Josephus, while he never actually embraced the Christian faith, not only testifies that a man named Jesus really lived; he also speaks of Him with awe and wonders whether Jesus were just a man.

Still another historical witness is Cerinthus, leader of a splinter group that drifted away from the early church and became a counter movement. Cerinthus holds that matter is inherently evil. Therefore, Jesus could not be God because God would not touch evil matter. So Cerinthus explains Jesus in other ways but repeatedly refers to "Jesus, the man from Nazareth." And so, while denying that "God became flesh," Cerinthus confirms that Jesus really lived.[9]

We have heard only a few from the chorus of ancient voices that could be summoned from secular history. But let us "rest our historical case" with the words of Albert Schweitzer from his book *The Quest of the Historical Jesus*. After years of cataloguing historical references to the man Jesus, Schweitzer concluded:

> It must be admitted that there are few characters of antiquity about whom we possess so much indubitably historical information, of whom we have so many authentic discourses. The position is much more favorable, for instance, than in the case of Socrates; for he is pictured to us by literary men who exercised their creative ability upon the portrait. Jesus stands much more immediately before us, because he was depicted by simple Christians without literary gift.[10]

We now call a second group of witnesses to the stand—not secular historians, but the actual writers of the New Testament themselves. You may object: "They were the crowd *trying* to sell their mythical Jesus as a real person. To quote them is to beg the question."

If I had been trying to sell people on some mythological, nonexistent person, I would be very careful what I wrote about him.

Fair enough. But keep in mind that Matthew, Mark, Luke, and John, the men who wrote the Gospels, were Jesus' contemporaries. Their original audience also consisted of Jesus' contemporaries, some of whom were his neighbors.

Now, if I had been trying to sell people on some mythological, nonexistent person, I would be very careful what I wrote about him. I would steer clear of anything that could be checked out. Wouldn't you? I would be vague. I certainly would not use places, dates, events, and names.

But the writers of the Gospels seem to expect their readers to check out their story. They fling down data as if to say, "Here are the facts. We invite investigation."

For example, Luke writes:

In the *sixth month*, God sent the angel *Gabriel* to *Nazareth*, a town in *Galilee*, to a *virgin* pledged to be married to a man named *Joseph*, a descendant of *David*. The virgin's name was *Mary*.[11]

Luke's facts are generous and specific: the month, the woman's name, her marital status, the man's name and tribe, the province and the city, even the angel's name.

Matthew lists Jesus' father's name and occupation (carpenter), His brothers' names (James, Joseph, Simon, Judas), His mother's name (Mary), and the fact that He had sisters.[12]

Keep in mind: Matthew knew some of his first readers would be locals. And still he seems to challenge: "All right. Go knock on doors and ask, 'Did a guy named Joseph live in this town?'

"'Yeah, he ran a carpenter shop down the street.'

"'His wife's name?'

"'Mary.'

"'Any kids?'

"'Yes. James, Joseph, Simon, Judas, Jesus, and some girls.'"

The readers could easily check these people out. And yet all four of the Gospel writers deliberately include reams of specific information. They tell us not only who Jesus was but also His hometown, where He walked and slept and ate, the names of His friends and His enemies, what made Him angry, and what made Him happy. They supply His father's name, His grandfather's name, His great-grandfather's name. They even trace His family tree back forty generations, all the way back to Adam.[13]

Now, really! Would someone care to rise and recite the family tree of Santa Claus? In order to deny that the man Jesus ever lived, I would have to either deny the facts or be unaware of them!

MORE THAN JUST A MAN

But Jesus' *human* existence is not the only issue, of course. In fact, many people who acknowledge that Jesus the man really lived and walked on earth do not believe He is the Son of God. Some who even acknowledge His goodness and His wisdom and claim to buy into His values don't see why it is important that they also believe in Jesus' divinity.

But there's a problem with that line of thinking: Jesus Himself made audacious claims about who He was and what He was about.

He said He was more than a good man and a wise teacher. In fact, He said He was the embodiment of God's truth, having broken into space and time in visible human form. That is why He said, "I am the way and the truth and the life," then added, "No one comes to the Father except through me." Jesus also said, "I am the bread of life" and "I am the light of the world." He even claimed, "I am the resurrection and the life."[14]

In fact, Jesus actually claimed to be God. So if Jesus was not who He claimed to be, He could not have been either wise or good. He would have to be either a lunatic or a liar.

But Jesus did back His claims with miraculous demonstrations of power. He healed blind, deaf, mute, and leprous people. He drove out demons and stilled storms with a word. Jesus even mastered death—first the death of His friend, Lazarus, then His own death. But beyond the miracles, Jesus validated His claims by His character. Jesus *was* what He taught. He underscored everything He said by living it out: "tempted in every way, just as we are—yet was without sin."[15]

Seventeenth-century apologist Joseph Glanvill put it this way:

'Tis not the doing of wonderful things that is the only evidence that the holy Jesus was from God...but the *conjunction of other circumstances*. The holiness of his life, the reasonableness of his religion, and the excellence of his designs, added credit to his works and strengthened the great conclusion, that he could be no other than the Son of God.[16]

Why Do We Need a Divine Jesus?

Even though the Bible clearly speaks of Jesus' divinity, you might ask, "But why do we need that? If I do what Jesus said to do, why is it important to believe that He was 'God come in the flesh'? Can't I just buy into His values and lead a good life without all this metaphysical stuff?"

Of course you can. In the short run. In the long run, however, I am convinced that you will be disappointed. The foundation for your values will not be equal to the challenges life will bring them. Besides, Jesus didn't come just to show us how to live a good life. The whole purpose of His coming was to meet our deepest human needs, needs that can't be met merely through a value system taught by a wise and good man. As the Bible says, "If only for this life we have hope in Christ, we are to be pitied more than all men."[17]

What are these needs that only a divine Christ, a Jesus who is God come in the flesh, can fill?

NEED #1: A DEPENDABLE RESTING PLACE

First, we need a Jesus who is not merely another man because almost everyone *is looking for a solid place to let down his or her weight.* We all need a dependable foundation for our values, indeed, for life's very purpose.

A doctor friend in Canada loved to talk sports. "You know," he observed, to my surprise, "I really liked the good old days before televised sports."

"What do you mean?" I asked.

He said, "You can't be certain about anything these days. But back before televised sports, you could count on one thing: *The umpire was always right.* Now, with instant replay, you can't even be sure about *that.*"

That's right. We hunger for a solid place to let down our weight and say, "This is true. I know it. And I can give my life to it. I don't have to feel confused anymore. I can live in confidence."

Some years ago, I was part of a panel of resource people at a high-school symposium on drug abuse. On my left sat a high-school senior, articulate and intelligent—but very much a part of the drug scene. He spoke openly of repeated experiences with hallucinogens and pot and coke. On my right sat a pharmacist and an attorney.

The attorney expounded the legal penalties for drug abuse. The pharmacist explained physical and emotional risks involved. The student made his reply. The audience sat silent except for bursts of uproarious laughter at the devastating one-liners from the lad on my left!

Since I was "resource," I was expected to say something, but I didn't know what it should be; frankly, I felt intimidated. Finally it struck me that we had never discussed the central issue: "*Why* do people take drugs anyway? Knowing the legal, physical, and psychological risks, why would anyone deliberately choose substance abuse as a lifestyle?"

Turning to the student on my left, I asked him that question.

At first he stared at me in mock surprise. Then he said, "Man, you gotta be bombed out of your birdie. Doin' drugs is where the whole thing is at! It is the *ultimate purpose for being human!*"

I couldn't argue with his logic. I told the audience, "That sounds like the right reason to me. Don't miss the ultimate purpose for being human. Whether it is doing drugs or kicking Grandma's dog—if it really is the ultimate purpose for being human, don't let your parents or the attorney or the politician or the preacher talk you out of it. *If! If!* If it really is the ultimate!"

But then I explained that I felt the young man had settled for too small an "ultimate." "I can think of an *ultimate* for life infinitely better than chemical highs! Not a *thing*. He is a person! He *didn't* live—He *does* live—He is alive in my own life now. And because He is, I know who I am, and life is going somewhere." I told the student that I was neither afraid to die nor afraid to live!

I recommended Jesus to the students. "You might not 'buy' Him. But be smart. Ignore the propaganda against Him and check the facts. Read the original documents about Jesus: Matthew, Mark, Luke, and John. If you still reject Him, then make sure to be fair with yourself and come up with an ultimate that is a whole lot better…if you can."

At this point, to my absolute astonishment, the audience broke into applause! In an ordinary plain old pagan high school, like the one you might have attended! I don't think the applause came because the kids were entertained or even because they were buying in to Jesus. Their applause meant I had touched a nerve. In fact, several told me afterward, "We don't know what life is for!"

But then a point of real insight came.

The lawyer with whom I had shared the podium stepped over to me and said, "Look, I'm going to level with you. I am an atheist! But I am not going to knock what you said to those kids—*everyone needs a crutch!*"

Again I felt bumfuzzled, but in my fumbling attempt to hold up my end of the conversation, words something like these tumbled out of my mouth: "Perhaps you are right. I don't think we human beings were designed to make it on our own. Maybe we do need crutches." Then, meeting his eyes, but still cautiously, I ventured to ask him, "What is your crutch?"

I might as well have punched that attorney in the solar plexus. His face dropped. He shuffled his feet and cleared his throat. I was beginning to feel embarrassed—first at what I had said, then at the silence that fell. We both felt shaken by the immense thoughts we had stumbled onto. Then he answered, "Well, I'll tell you—I stay real busy!"

In that pregnant moment we both stood on the rim, staring into the yawning canyon of a despair that contrasts starkly with Christian hope. He, too, sensed the emptiness, I think. Maybe he had for a long time. He had said he kept "busy." I wondered if he meant that he kept moving fast enough so that the wind roaring in his ears would drown out the inner voices that kept asking those giant questions: Why? What for? Where is the solid place to let down my weight? Without a solid foundation, why is law important?

We stood on the rim, staring into the yawning canyon of a despair that contrasts starkly with Christian hope.

And what does it matter if we damage brains and bodies with drugs—if we are only high-grade amoebas?

God designed us and knows what makes us tick. And if He says, "This is the way life ought to be lived," His advice will be solid. We *can* let our weight down on that! This is the kind of foundation we need for our values—and for life itself. Not just a word of human wisdom—but straight talk from our Maker, from God Himself! If Jesus is God, His way will be rock solid.

Helen Young, wife of Norvel Young—long-time chancellor of Pepperdine University—says her faith in Jesus feels to her like a big, comfortable, strong bed. At the end of an exhausting day, she simply falls into bed. Ah—relief! She doesn't let her weight down gingerly, wondering if the bed will hold her. No, she flops down wholeheartedly, secure the frame will support her as it always has. And she doesn't worry all night, "I wonder if this bed will hold up. I think I feel it collapsing. I'd better hang on." Rather, she rests completely secure on that bed.

We all long to rest the weight of life on One who is worthy of our trust! And only if Jesus is God can we know that He is truly dependable.

NEED #2: A WAY TO GET PAST GUILT

The need for a dependable foundation for our values and our lives isn't the only reason we need a divine Jesus. In addition, consciously or unconsciously, we are desperate for a Savior who *can wash away our sins*. We don't really want someone to sweep things under the rug or to convince us nothing is wrong—we *know* something's radically wrong. We know we are guilty. We carry around loads of guilt and remorse and self-deprecation—sometimes so much that we have to deny it just to get through the day.

"All have sinned."[18] That's the bad news—and it's not really news. What we need is some good news—a way to put things right. Forgiveness. And that forgiveness is available *only in Jesus Christ*.

Only the blood of Jesus, God's only Son, can make things right again. Only His blood can wash away our sins and guilt.[19] When it comes to handling our deep-down guilt and giving us the chance to start over clean, only the Son of God will do.

Think of it this way:

You are standing in a courtroom before an awesome judge. You have just been rightly convicted of a serious crime and sentenced to pay a fine of five thousand dollars. If you do not pay now, you will be sentenced to years in prison. But you do not have a cent to your name, and you have no means of getting that kind of money.

The judge's gavel falls! In despair, you drop your eyes. What are you going to do?

Then you hear a commotion near the bench. You look up and see that the judge who sentenced you has just stepped down. He is taking off his robe and moving toward you. And now, standing right beside you, he takes out his wallet and pays your fine—every cent!

This is exactly what God did on the cross. He paid the full price for our crimes—and that price was to bear our penalty for us. Christ was treated as we deserve so that we might be treated as He deserves. He died for our sins, in which He had no part, so that we could be justified by His righteousness in which we had no part. He died the death that belongs to us so that we might live the life that belongs to Him.

Isaiah the prophet was not exaggerating when he wrote,

> Surely he took up our infirmities and carried our sorrows.... He was pierced for our transgressions, he was crushed for our iniquities; the punishment that brought us peace was upon him, and by his wounds we are healed.... The LORD has laid on him the iniquity of us all. [20]

Why did it have to be a divine Jesus? No one else is good enough to be able to pay the price for his or her own sins, let alone all other people's sins as well. God selected the only offering worth enough to pay, in that one event, the penalty of all the sins of all human beings in history. The only One worth that much was Jesus, God's sinless Son. He alone could pay our debt and open up for us the way to forgiveness.

NEED #3: AN END TO OUR ESTRANGEMENT FROM GOD

Yet another reason we need a divine Jesus is that *we need some-one to bring us back home to God*. We need to be reconciled to Him. And that, too, happens only through Jesus.

If I were to steal your car, I would make you my enemy. You might not know I had stolen it. But my heart would say, "People don't steal cars from friends. No, he *has* to be my enemy." That is human nature! Just so, we broke from God. We often regard Him as a cosmic enemy, even though *we* are the ones who wronged *Him*.

But God does not deal in vendetta. He loves us and wants us to come back to Him. But how? Lightning bolts? A thunderous voice from the sky? Warnings in the night? Any attempt to force us back would only more thoroughly convince us that He is our enemy! So God has to woo us back to Him.

To illustrate: George came home from work angry. Mary said something he didn't like. George said harsh words. Mary defended herself. George retaliated and really cussed her out. The streams of verbal abuse poured out before he stormed out the front door.

> Jesus came down to our dark streets to tell us the Father still loves us and longs for us to come home!

But before he was halfway down the street George was raking himself over the coals: "Why did I do that to the woman I love? I have never done anything like this before in my life. But I did it. Now she will *never* have anything to do with me again. You don't treat a woman like that and expect her to stay with you." With that, George headed down the street, around the corner into the bar to chemically reinforce his imaginary picture of Mary's rage.

But Mary wasn't angry. "That was not my husband," she reflected. "He isn't like that. I don't want this incident to damage our marriage."

So she ran down the street calling, "George, come back!"

In George's addled state he only heard Mary screaming threats. Mary called the bar, but George wouldn't come to the phone.

"She wants to send the sheriff down here so they can put me in jail. Do you know what I did to that woman?"

Their four-year-old daughter, Heather, couldn't help taking in the whole drama. Mary tried all day to reach George, but to no avail. Finally, night fell.

In desperation, Mary turned to Heather, "I want you to go down with me to that part of town where I don't even like you to go in the daytime. I know it's dangerous. But I want you to go in that bar and tell Daddy that we love him and we want him to come home."

Heather was scared, but when they got to the bar, she let go of her mother's hand, walked into the joint, and found her daddy.

George was still suspicious, "Did your mother send you to spite me?" But Heather wrapped her tiny arms around Daddy's neck.

"No, Daddy! Mommy sent me in here to say we love you. We want you to come home."

Then Heather led George out the door and into the warm embrace of *reconciliation!*

This is what God did on the cross—through Jesus!

God watched us run from Him. "How will I tell them I love them? How? Their ears are so full of rebellion and guilt that they cannot hear my voice. How will I call them back home?" So the Father said, "My Son, I want you to go down into that world where you can be destroyed." (One cannot be tempted to do what he cannot do, yet the Bible says Jesus was "tempted in every way, just as we are."[21])

Jesus came down to our dark streets to tell us the Father still loves us and longs for us to come home! "For God was pleased... through him to reconcile to himself all things...by making peace through his blood, shed on the cross."[22]

And it had to be Jesus! Jesus was the only way God could get through to us.

Let me show it a little more vividly. Imagine we are in Jerusalem the day Jesus died. What is that? Someone knocking on the door?

"Hey, come with me out to Golgotha. There's a crucifixion going on."

"Again? Bah, you know these Romans. If you've seen one crucifixion, you've seen them all."

"No, no. This one is different. This man says that he is dying for God."

"Well, who is God mad at this time?" (This would be my reaction to news of the crucifixion of a Jesus who is simply another man—even a wise and good man.)

"You don't understand. This one says that *He is God.*"

So we follow down the street and up to the hill. The sky has turned black by the time we arrive at the cross; the earth is trembling, and rocks are cracking open. Lightning lashes the hill like a strobe light, fixing Jesus' face in a sequence of freeze-framed images as He calls out, "Father—forgive them—because they don't know what they are doing—into your hands—I commit my spirit."

Silhouetted against the lightning, a Roman soldier falls to his knees in acknowledgment: "This was the *Son of God!*"

When I understand what God has done in Jesus on the cross, my perspective changes. The estrangement ends. I understand that God isn't my enemy. He loves me—enough to die for me! That is how much He wants me back home.

This is why, for centuries, the message, "Christ died for me," has led men and women to fall at the foot of His cross. Only a cross with a crucified God on it closes the gap between God and His estranged children.

But once again, the man on the cross had to be the Son of God. The death of another man would only incite more resentment toward God. The death of an angel would go unnoticed in our world. But when God's Son broke into my world and died on a cross, that means something.

As Paul the apostle put it, "Once you were alienated from God and were enemies in your minds because of your evil behavior. But now he has reconciled you by Christ's physical body through death to present you holy in his sight.... This is the gospel that you heard and that has been proclaimed to every creature."[23]

NEED #4: A GOD WHO KNOWS OUR NAME

Finally, we need Jesus because we long *for a warm friend who never leaves us.* We need a God who knows our name.

I am an alcoholic—albeit an honorary one. Over the years, I visited many A.A. meetings and established friendships with some of the nicest people I know. In fact, I became so attached that one evening, even though I was not a drinker, I said, "I wish there were some way I could join this organization, since I have so many friends here. Do I need to throw a binge to qualify?"

"Oh no," they chorused. "We'll make you an honorary member."

So now, when I go to A.A. meetings, I say, "My name is Lynn, and I am an *honorary* alcoholic."

Well, I met the Harders at an A.A. meeting when we lived in Canada. The Harders were both alcoholics. Alf was on the wagon, dry for over two years now. Elsie was just making her first run at it and had over five months of sobriety under her belt. The Harders and their beautiful children started attending our church. Then Elsie asked me if I would take the "fifth step" with her, which is the step where you "admit to God, ourselves, and one other human being the exact nature of our wrongs."

I was glad to, and Elsie did great till her first big fall. Boom! She disappeared one day. Word went out that she had gotten drunk and run off with Harvey from the nearby Indian Reservation. Harvey, also an alcoholic, had a violent history. He was on parole from prison, where he had been doing time for assaulting three Mounties.

Alf found out where Elsie and Harvey were staying. He said she would listen to me. He asked me to go see if she would come home to him and the kids.

When I drove up in front of the motel where I had heard Harvey and Elsie were living, Harvey was nowhere to be seen, but Elsie walked outside. She was cordial and agreed to talk. So we got in the car and had begun a hopeful conversation when a taxi drove up and out rolled Harvey.

Now, I have seen Harvey three times, but only once sober; and this was definitely not the sober time. He saw me in the car with Elsie, and I guess he figured I was boyfriend number three. So he charged the car, trying to yank open the door, and drew a huge knife. (Actually, it was a tiny pocket penknife, with an inch and a half of dull blade, but to me it looked like the sword of a Samurai.)

Elsie lifted my Bible to the window, and for some reason that gesture stalled Harvey. He calmed some and invited me in to talk— an invitation I was not disposed to decline.

> If Jesus were just a man, His love would not be pure enough, strong enough, or deep enough to fill our need for divine love.

Once inside, Harvey began to pour out his life story of communal alcoholism and violent abuse, both verbal and physical. Part of the time, Harvey would press the point of his knife to my chin and threaten to "cut my innards out." But most of the time he was on his knees with his arms around my legs begging for help.

"My old man always told me I was no good," remembered Harvey, "and he was right. He used to say, 'Harvey, no one will ever like you, no one will ever love you—not me, not even your mother. Because you are no good.'"

Even if Harvey had offered me the opportunity to leave, I am not sure I would have been able to. After a couple of hours had passed, Harvey sobered up enough that the incoherence and violence died away. I put my hands on his shoulders and said, "Harvey, do you understand what I am saying to you? You don't have to do this to yourself and to other people, because there is a God who knows your name."

"Naw, I'm just a drunk Indian."

"You are a human being, Harvey, made in the image of God. He knows you and loves you. In fact, He loves you so much that if you had been the only person in the universe, He would still have sent His Son, Jesus, to die for you."

Harvey looked up at me with what seemed to me a startled

expression, "Why, I ain't never heard nothin' like that in my whole life!"

Two weeks later was the next time I saw Harvey. I was speaking at a gathering of A.A. groups from around the area on the occasion of the birthday of the founder. When I stood to speak, I couldn't believe my eyes. There sat Harvey—clear-eyed, clean-shaven, and dressed in a suit and tie. As soon as I could get to him afterwards, I walked up and spoke: "Harvey."

He said, "Do I know you?"

So I put my hands on his shoulders and said, "Harvey, there is a God who knows your name…"

"Oh, so you're the guy. Listen, what you said hit me harder than anything I have ever heard. And you know what? I haven't had a drink since that afternoon. Longest sober streak I've had since I was a kid."

That was the last time I saw Harvey, because we moved to Texas the next week. I wish I knew what happened from there. But I'll never forget what that one simple statement did for Harvey.

Make sure you hear my point. I am not suggesting that process as a one-shot cure for alcoholism. (Usually, support groups such as A.A. are God's most effective tools for that.) But I am saying there is tremendous power in knowing that we are personally loved by Almighty God and that Jesus offers us hope and dignity. Harvey said it rocked his world more than anything he had ever heard.

This is what people need. Not just to believe there is a creative force on the backside of space, but to know we matter to a loving God who is very near.

As Buechner says, we are not just wanting a mind behind "the steely brightness of the stars."[24] We want a relationship with a God who knows our names, who walks these uneven roads with us.

But it *is* God who walks these roads with us. Jesus is not merely a compassionate man. He is a compassionate God who came near and brought His love in human form, with skin on it. If Jesus were just a man, His love would not be pure enough, strong enough, or deep enough to fill our need for divine love.

TARGETING YOUR FAITH

What is the object of your faith? It *really* does matter what you believe! Or, more important, *whom* you believe.

Let Jesus be the object of your faith. Jesus is God; thus He is the solid place to let down your weight, the One who can wash away your sins, the One who will bring you home, the warm friend who knows your name and will never leave you.

He is not far away. As we step toward Him on the road of faith, He is eager to come and meet us. And those to whom He comes know that life will never be the same.

> I shall know Him when He comes,
> Not by any din of drums,
> Nor by the vantage of His airs,
> Nor by anything He wears;
> Neither know Him by His crown,
> Neither know Him by His gown,
> But His presence known shall be
> By the holy harmony
> Which His coming makes in me.[25]

So if you want your faith to grow, decide on a faith commitment. Surround yourself with people who believe. Clarify the object of your faith: Jesus Christ, the Son of the living God. Examine the *evidence* pointing toward Him as the object of faith. Reflect on His *worthiness* as the object of faith. Keep on getting to know *Him*. (Chapter 10 will give you some handles on how to do that.) And as you get to know Him better and better, your former indifference to Him will be radically transformed. His life will bring a new vitality to your life.

Feeding
Faith

A fourth step toward faith…
is to feed one's mind with faith-building material.

My friend Ted decided that during his Sunday-school years he had been brainwashed in favor of the Christian faith. So when he headed off to university, Ted said, "Well, I grew up in church and went to Sunday school all of my life. I've *heard* the case for Christianity. Now I want to hear the other side. I want to read all the books I can find by the best minds among unbelievers."

Bingo! Before long, Ted became a practical unbeliever.

No mystery! Ted's doubts grew because he put *doubt-building material* in his mind.

CHOOSE YOUR THOUGHTS

Believe it or not, a person does choose the kind of thoughts he or she thinks. Our thoughts come from what we put in our heads. If you decide you want to believe and then feed your mind faith-building material, you will become a believer. If, on the other hand, you choose to feed your mind a steady diet of doubt-building material, you will become an unbeliever! It is almost that simple.

If you really want to be an unbeliever, you can find plenty of powerful literature to help you confirm that choice. You may want to begin with Mark Twain's *Letters from the Earth*, in which Twain says, "Special providence! The phrase nauseates me. God doesn't know that we are here, and would not care if He did."[1] Or try Bertrand Russell's book *Why I Am Not a Christian*. It will blow your doors off.

Ted read both of those books—and others. But Ted wasn't really playing fair. The Sunday schools in which he had grown up were staffed by poorly informed teachers in less than effective educational situations. Theology preached from the pulpit of Ted's youth lacked relevance and depth. Nevertheless, he flung the flimsy theology of Sunday-school faith into a life-and-death showdown with university-level doubt. There was no contest!

If you want to explore alternatives to faith, be sure you are being fair with yourself about it. Explore the best thinking available on *both* sides. You do not have to look far for excellent faith-building material. Two of the best faith building-blocks out there are by Lee Strobel, formerly an atheist and legal affairs reporter for the *Chicago Tribune*, but now a widely read Christian writer. His two faith builders are *The Case for Christ* and *The Case for Faith*. Other excellent faith-building materials are listed in the appendix.

And once you have decided that you definitely do want to believe, then make a point of putting faith-building material into your mind. Faith-building material includes books, tapes, conversations, movies, radio and television programs, music, and other messages that:

- encourage your faith
- enrich your understanding of God
- guide you in forming a Christian lifestyle
- help you examine intellectual obstacles to faith
- supply you with evidence supportive of faith

- press you for integrity of heart
- lead you farther into your personal relationship with God

THE PRIMARY SOURCE

Of course, the primary source of faith-building material is the Bible. Scripture aids faith by shaping a wholesome and attractive view of God! As the apostle Paul put it in his letter to the Romans, "Faith comes by hearing, and hearing by the word of God."[2]

> When God says something and we act on it, the Word validates itself in our experience.

But how does faith come by hearing the words of Scripture? Is this a brainwashing technique—listen to something often enough and you begin to believe it?

Brainwashing can work that way; Adolf Hitler kept repeating portions of *Mein Kampf* until he brainwashed a nation. But this is not what Paul means. Nor does he mean that vast biblical knowledge will necessarily produce faith. We can have our brains pickled on biblical information and still not develop a personal, trusting relationship with God. I know several agnostics who hold doctorates in biblical literature!

No, Paul goes on to distinguish between simply "hearing" and "knowing" or "understanding."[3] It's the difference between *reading* and *heeding*. And it is in heeding the Word of God that our faith grows.

And what happens when we really hear the Word of God? When God says something and we act on it, the Word validates itself in our experience.

Scripture promises, for example, in Psalm 1, that the person whose "delight is in the law of the Lord" and who "meditates [on it] day and night" will eventually be blessed with a fruitful life. Great idea—but how can I know if this idea is true? By acting on it! And as I do—as I meditate and delight in the Word, eventually the fruit of the Spirit does begin to appear in my life. Then I *know* it is true. The Word of God is self-validating.

The Word validates itself in another way too. The Word targets our feelings through what I call "Aha!" experiences.

We all treasure many private feelings that are very real to us yet so complex and enormously personal that we can find no words to explain them, even if we wanted to. Certain fears. Special temptations. Little joys. Twanging pains. Rushes of emotion. The sound of an old song awakens a whole world of sleeping memories. A fragrance triggers explosions of nostalgia or pain. A face from the past stirs old, personal mysteries.

Constellations of these feelings crowd daily experience. I had considered dropping in an example of such an experience at this point. But after days of scribbling and coming up empty, I feel a bit embarrassed that I missed the obvious. How can I give you an example of something that is so private, complex, and enormously personal that it defies words? If I could find words to describe it so that you could understand, then it could not be the kind of experience I am talking about. However, by now I suspect you understand quite well what I mean, and you are already recalling some of your own. You have them, too, right?

I didn't realize how important I am to God—and that He actually might be counting on me.

Sometimes Scripture intersects with these undescribables. As you are reading along in the Bible, one insight brushes against another as both converge with one of those personal mysteries and—bingo!— we get an "Aha!" experience. The Word of God probes these private places on multiple fronts, penetrating "soul and spirit, joints and marrow," even judging "the thoughts and attitudes of the heart."[4]

The first few times this comes as a surprise: "Aha! I thought this book was written by mere fishermen, farmers, and tax collectors. Yet two thousand years ago they wrote things that precisely resonate with my heart and diagnose my twenty-first–century psyche. How did those ancients have such accurate insight into modern life?"

But after a while, we come to expect the "Aha!" experience and even to look for it. The living Word of God sharply probes these subtle nuances and articulates private experiences that we ourselves could not express. The longer we live in the Word of God, the more fresh and private insight we gain, and the more the "Aha!" comes to us!

Some time ago, Ruth sat in our living room. She had come to our house directly from the hospital, where she had been recovering from yet another suicide attempt. Rejected by her family years before, Ruth had become a Christian and struggled on alone. Then Ruth had fallen into a destructive codependent relationship. Eventually her boyfriend had abandoned her. Now she felt guilt-ridden, dirty, and worthless.

Ruth said she was afraid to go home for fear she would destroy herself. She even said, "I can see absolutely no reason to live. I am worth nothing to anyone. If God really does love me—then, surely He wouldn't care if I kill myself."

At almost that moment, my three-year-old son bounced around the corner. When their eyes met, a smile of pure sunshine broke across her face and everything in her responded, reached for him. Of course, he beamed back at her.

Then came the spark of hope. I said, "There's no way I could tell you how much I love that little boy—and you just made him smile. I appreciate anyone who brings richer happiness to my son. Now, God has hundreds of children all over the world. He loves them more than I ever could love my son. He wants them happy. And He loves them so much that the Bible says 'He gave His only Son'[5] for them. He has given you—each of us—a unique way to make His children smile.

"If you destroy yourself, you will actually block God's love for you and for everyone your life could touch. You will destroy a reflection of God Himself, and you will rob some of His children of the smile God sent them through you."

I think this was an "Aha!" for Ruth. Several days later, still mildly depressed but doing much better, Ruth said, "I think I will make it now. I didn't realize how important I am to God—and that He actually might be counting on me. I don't feel like a non-person anymore. I have begun visiting a psychologist. And I find myself thinking a lot about God again. I have hope!"

This "Aha!" experience—this "Bingo!" moment when something deep in God's Word connected with something deep in Ruth—was the moment when she caught a glimpse of the "Godness" in herself. Her *belief about* God was becoming *faith in* God!

This "Aha!" phenomenon has occurred so many times in my life that an almost inescapable web of faith has woven itself around my heart. Scripture has validated itself over and over again in my own life. I have *experienced* these truths, so I know their truth! "Unanswerable" challenges no longer threaten my faith because I *know* it is true. I have experienced the truth of it. Faith has come by hearing the Word—and knowing it! (These faith-building qualities of Scripture are described in more detail in chapter 11.)

OTHER RESOURCES

However, the Bible is by no means the only faith-building resource available. Some of the finest minds of the centuries have written volumes elaborating the reasons they believe and providing insight into faith.

An annotated list of faith-building material is supplied in the appendix, with suggestions for possible beginning places. Some fine works are now available on multiple media—music, videos, tapes, books, and over the radio. The books and tapes on my list run the gamut from elementary to scholarly.

No matter what level of interest you may have, ample faith-building resources stand ready to spring into action for you at any speed you wish to travel or on whatever level your interest runs. But you are in charge. You *do* control what your mind thinks. In fact, if you want to believe, then you are the only one who can choose to invite this faith-building material into your mind.

Choose to read faith-building books. Listen to good faith-building tapes. Watch helpful Christian videos. Plug Christian music into your stereo. Tune in your radio to good faith-building music. Initiate faith-building conversations. You can consistently choose to do that.

PRAYER AS A RESOURCE

Would you consider prayer a form of feeding one's mind faith-building material? I would—if you escape the trap of using prayer only as an opportunity to tell God what to do. If you approach prayer from a healthy perspective, prayer can be a source of valuable input from the living Word; and the very process of spending time with God can build faith as well.

But prayer is a problem for some of us doubters. Sometimes we may feel as if no one is listening. Or we may be afraid to ask for anything, because we have done that before and it accomplished nothing. Sometimes we might even feel a little silly, sitting alone in a room talking out loud to Someone who is invisible and never seems to hold up His end of the conversation (if, indeed, He is there at all).

Maybe this is because we expect God to answer in certain ways; if He doesn't, we doubt. But I believe God always answers our prayers, one way or another. Bill Hybels quotes a friend who describes God's answers this way:

- If the request is wrong, God says, "No."
- If the time is wrong, God says, "Slow."
- If *you* are wrong, God says, "Grow."
- But if the request is right, the timing is right, and you are right, God says, "Go."[6]

Praying will certainly not feed your faith if you assume the primary purpose of prayer is to *talk to God*, especially to ask Him for things. Prayer also means *listening to God*. Sometimes I stay on the request line so much that when God tries to get through, I'm sure He gets a busy signal. Our "talky" prayers may leave Him wondering if He will ever get His say.

But when we get still before Him in prayer, God does speak to us. How? He speaks through His Word, when a surprising but timely and much-needed insight jumps off the page at us or emerges in our memory. He speaks His love and care in the words or actions of an affirming or listening friend. He guides through the probing questions of a caring fellow believer or the example of someone we deeply respect. He even speaks through what seems bitter disappointment.

However, God also speaks through more direct promptings. Scripture maintains that believers are "controlled by the [Holy] Spirit"; thus they are to "live by the Spirit," to be "led by the Spirit," to "keep in step with the Spirit," and to *pray in the Spirit* on all occasions."[7] Although these "prayer promptings" from the Spirit may be too subjective to publicize and, of course, must be checked against Scripture, they are nonetheless real and important in feeding our faith. Over time, as we act on these promptings, we gain confidence in them; we come to recognize and trust a familiar voice.

God's ultimate purpose in prayer is to bring us to Himself.

Actually, the meaning of prayer runs much deeper than laying requests before God or even listening to God—and understanding this deeper meaning can help clear up some of prayer's problematic aspects. God's ultimate purpose in prayer is to bring us to Himself. He will do whatever is necessary—even allowing us to suffer—to achieve that purpose.

In a sense, then, prayer (including "unanswered prayer") is the arena in which we win the struggle between God's will and our wills; no wonder it is often an arena of turmoil.

Paul the apostle prayed three times about some besetting problem, "God take it from me." And God answered three times, "Keep it. You need it to learn that I am enough for you."[8] God was involved in Jesus' prayer life, too, but that did not prevent weeping, pain, discouragement, humiliation, or even death. Jesus prayed for His father to release Him from death. And His father answered with a cross!

What, then, of the Bible verses that promise direct answers to prayers?[9] These verses are reassurances of God's purpose. They are reminding us that God does answer and there is not anything He will not do to bring us to Himself. There is no mountain He cannot move, no miracle He cannot perform, no resource He would withhold to help us achieve oneness with Him.

If a child asks her father, "Will you give me everything I want?" the father will answer no.

"What *will* you give me?"

The father will answer, "My child, I will give you *everything!*"

So with God.

Yes, there are times when the whole question of prayer seems to feed our doubts. If we put our trust in getting out of God anything we ask for, we will be disappointed. We may even lose our faith in prayer—or maybe even in God. But prayer will nourish our faith if we look for His purposes rather than our wishes. In the words of Katharina von Schlegel:

> Be still my soul,
> Thy best, thy heavenly friend,
> Through thorny ways
> Leads to a joyful end![10]

If you are still not convinced, don't take my word for it. Instead, watch praying people carefully. What you will find, I predict, is that those who stay at it the longest tend to be the ones who believe the most deeply. And they will tell you from their own experience: Time spent in prayer will feed your faith.

TRANSPORTABLE SOLITUDE

Delving into faith-building material—whether Scripture, prayer, or other resources—is most easily done in solitude, away from the distractions of everyday life. I can think of no better faith builder than to get away periodically to a retreat center or even a hotel room for an afternoon, a weekend, or even a week of silent reading and reflection.

But that kind of solitude is hard to come by—and silence

sometimes next to impossible. It is not easy to concentrate regularly on faith-building things while at the same time remaining part of the twenty-first century, but it can be done. Henri Nouwen, a leading writer on the inner life, is a good example.[11] Although he writes about prayer and reflection, he lives not in a desert monastery but in a noisy city. As a busy priest and professor with several side interests, he has discovered solitude as a transportable state of mind and heart rather than a geographic location.

A number of hurried Christians I know are coming up with creative ways to get transportable solitude for faith nourishment without a sense of adding to already overburdened daily schedules. Here are some ideas:

- Drive time is valuable. Michelle and several other California commuters have covenanted among themselves to use drive time for reflection. They leave their radios off and listen only to faith-invigorating tapes they circulate among themselves. Or they simply mark off the time for prayer and contemplation. Michelle calls her car "my mobile monastery." (See the appendix for some helpful tape suggestions.)

- David, whose doctor handed him an ultimatum sounding like "daily exercise or death," reads the Bible or other Christian literature while he rides his stationary bicycle. Other times he methodically works through his prayer list while jogging. I hear from a lot of joggers and walkers who do as David does! Some find a buddy and turn their exercise periods into joint prayer and discussion time.

- Traveling business people sit on a gold mine of faith development time aboard airplanes and in hotel rooms. Mac, whose face recently smiled from the front page of *The Wall Street Journal*, packs a special folder in his briefcase for "road reading." He also claims that keeping a journal at the end of the day keeps his faith and his work in perspective.

- Regina doesn't mind mowing her large yard. In fact, she

cannot wait to mount her riding mower with her portable stereo loaded with tapes of Scripture readings or Christian music or her mind filled with a prayer agenda. The chore melts away, and Regina's spirits soar.

Most Christian advisors would agree that feeding the mind is vital to growing faith. And this may require concerted effort. But let me sound a warning: Beware the temptation to fill all the cracks in our schedules with faith-building activity and wring all we can from the tag ends of time. Scrounging time for faith nourishment can press a doubter into *drivenness*—so that in our wild attempts to make the most of every minute of our time, we may lose eternity.

Yet no matter how cluttered our calendars may be, we dare not neglect feeding our faith. We must carve out time to listen for God's voice through His Word and the insights of fellow believers. A little creativity can go a long way in helping us find and enjoy those profitable times.

No Neutral Ground

If you do not choose to put faith-building materials in your mind, the choice will be made for you. A powerful secular environment will automatically invade your head with doubt-building material in a thousand forms. Every day the media bombards us with celebrities who laugh at God. Our radios scream out lyrics that applaud violence and greed and lust. Some movies, TV programs, and magazines glorify money, sex, and power. Others degrade women, ridicule men, exploit children, and poke fun at faith. Madison Avenue propaganda will also come at you from billboards, TV commercials, journals, and even T-shirts promoting still more greed, selfishness, violence, and lust. And all of these will look attractive, sophisticated, and right!

Make no mistake about it. The thoughts in our heads will not remain neutral. Neglect faith, and doubt will win by default.

The choice is simple. Decide to believe or not to believe, then feed the mind the material that supports your choice.

Too mechanical? Admittedly, it sounds that way. But those are the choices before you.

Well, actually there is one other option: You can decide not to decide, which really is a decision too. However, those who spend their lives straddling a fence are the most unfulfilled people I know. They go through life wanting two things at once and, at the same time, wanting neither one of them.

Fence-sitters suffer like my senior-citizen friend who says she has tremors so bad she can't keep still and arthritis so bad she can't stand to move! Or they are like the poor guy my friend Mid used to tell about who couldn't decide. He woke up at midnight. The temperature had dropped, and his house was so cold that his single blanket wouldn't keep him warm. But if he left the half-warmth of his bed to get a quilt, he would be even colder. The very thought made him shiver. So he spent the rest of the night too cold to sleep but not cold enough to get up and find more blankets. Indecision made him miserable.

Tony Campolo tells of a student who got trapped on the fence. Charlie was well known on campus as one who had no time for church or Bible study groups, who ridiculed Christians, who often went out barhopping and was openly promiscuous.

One evening after Tony had spoken at a church away from campus, Charlie's mother came up and introduced herself and asked if Tony knew her son. He did. The mother went on to tell how her son was active in the church youth group and led Bible studies in the summer months. It seemed everyone in his home church thought she was lucky to have such a wonderful son.

Back on campus, Tony confronted Charlie with what had happened: "You're a completely different person at home with those church people, aren't you?" Charlie's head dropped in shame.

The following semester, Charlie dropped by Tony's office and said, "Dr. Campolo, remember that talk we had last year? Well, you were right; I was being phony. But it's different now. I want you to know that this summer I never attended church once."

Though the behavior Charlie chose wasn't exactly what his professor had in mind, Tony wrote, "Charlie was getting closer to the kingdom of God than ever before." Charlie understood clearly that *he* was making a choice! When he got off the fence, at least he was being honest about his choices, even though he chose the road to unbelief.[12]

Once again, then, keeping on the road of faith is a matter of choosing:

- Decide whether you really want to believe.
- Go where faith is.
- Clarify the object of your faith.
- Choose to put faith-building material in your mind.

And then launch out into step five. Read on...

Doing Faith

11

A fifth step toward faith…
is to do what faith would do and
thus begin (or continue) one's experiment of faith.

Question: How many people in your circle can ride a bicycle? Almost everyone, you say?

Second question: How many learned how by reading a book, watching a video, or attending a seminar on that subject? None? Really? Aren't these standard learning channels for the current generation? Not when it comes to bike riding. Right? You had to climb on the thing and start pedaling. At first you scraped your knee and dented your pride. Then, gradually, you wobbled off into the hang of it. And no book, video, or seminar would have gotten you there.

In some ways, faith comes much like this. Theory won't get you there. You have to climb on the thing! You have to move out into faith. You must commit to doing what faith would do. Eventually you will discover that the behavior and values required by faith fit the reality of your experience. Gradually you will gather momentum toward faith, although at times you may feel like a wobbly believer.

THE EXPERIMENT OF FAITH

Now, doing what faith would do does not mean faking it and *pretending* to be a believer. I know one rah-rah type of spiritual cheerleader who used to quip, "Fake it till you make it!" This is not what I have in mind here! I am not suggesting that you claim to have achieved moral and ethical qualities that are larger than the realities of your life. But I do mean shoot for something bigger than what you now have. Try out the ways of the Christian faith. Begin your experiment of faith. Do what faith would do.

You remember your class on the scientific method from high school. You don't? Well, seems I recall it went something like this: Form your hypothesis (your theory), then test your hypothesis by experiment.

For example, you might theorize that if *a* mixes with *b* in manner *c*, then *d* will be the result. But that's still only a theory. Then you proceed with your experiment. You mix *a* with *b* in manner *c*, and when *d* results, you would say you were coming closer to validating your theory.

In a sense this technique applies to faith in God as well. By "experimenting" with faith—doing what faith would do—you come closer to validating your "theory" about God.

But doing what faith would do is more than just testing a theory.

> Doing what faith would do is more than just testing a theory.

Jesus said, "If you hold to my teaching, then you are really my disciples. Then you will know the truth, and the truth will set you free."[1] To teach, Jesus did not build a university; He simply started off walking and talking and inviting friends to follow. And those who *walked* with Him, *listening* to what He said, *doing* what He did, He called "disciples," which literally means "following learners."

Jesus still operates this way. Holding to His teaching is not just listening to it but doing it. If you proceed to follow Jesus and daily implement His teachings into your life, you become a disciple. You will be following and learning—even if it is at a somewhat experimental level. But as time passes, you will come to *"know the truth."*

By this, Jesus did not mean "you will understand all truth." He was saying "you will experience *a relationship* with truth."

"Knowledge" for the Greeks was acquired information. For the Hebrews, however, "knowing" meant experiencing. When the Bible says, "Adam knew Eve his wife,"[2] it does not mean that he merely possessed information about her existence but that he had experienced intimacy with her. So Jesus is saying that if we walk in His teachings, even with our doubts, sooner or later we will come to know that His teachings are true; we will experience the reality and relevance of their truth in our lives. More important, in time, we will begin to experience relationship with the One who is truth.

TASTING IS BELIEVING

Or, to look at experience from another angle…

Question: How do you talk a person into believing in God?

Answer: You can't!

Question: How do you prove there is a God?

Same answer!

In chapter 3 we observed that no one can make another person believe. No one can *prove* to you that God exists or that God cares about you or that God has a plan for your life. The only way you can come to that kind of faith is by choosing to open yourself to experiencing God firsthand. And you do that—once again—by stepping out and doing what faith would do.

Imagine trying to convince a friend that rainbows are beautiful when your friend has never seen a rainbow and refuses even to open her eyes and look at one.

"Why do you say it is beautiful?" she might ask.

"It's loaded with color," you explain.

"What colors?" she challenges.

"Red and blue and green and…"

"I don't like blue and green together!"

"They look good in rainbows."

"Why should I take your word for it?"

On the argument might go—unless, of course, your friend wanted to see a rainbow badly enough to actually look at one. And then, no doubt, she would believe, for there is something about rainbows that makes anyone who sees them stand in awe. I have never met anyone who thought rainbows were ugly. Have you?

Until your friend has experienced a rainbow, no argument will suffice. Once she has experienced a rainbow, no argument will be needed. She will believe because she has seen its splendor!

Just so (changing the metaphor), you must "taste that the Lord is good"[3] in order to genuinely believe in His goodness. Then once you have had a taste, you won't need a lot of further explanation. For your faith in God to flourish, you must taste, know, trust, and obey—not just abstractly believe in Him.

Faith Acts

Biblical faith is not merely a mental intellectual exercise akin to believing there are rings around Saturn. Although I do believe those rings exist, that faith in Saturn's rings has almost nothing to do with anything real in my experience at this moment. It is just an intellectual assent. And it's definitely not the relationship with God that the Bible describes as faith.

In fact, the Bible specifically comments on that kind of faith. James writes in his Epistle: "Someone will say, 'You have faith; I have deeds.' Show me your faith without deeds, and I will show you my faith by what I do."[4]

James does not mean that the deeds have any saving power in themselves or that our efforts can in any way ingratiate us with God. Rather, he is saying that real faith does more than accept or even trust; it *acts*.

He continues, "You believe there is one God [that God is out there like the rings around Saturn]. That's just great." However, "the demons believe that—and shudder," but they just keep on being little devils![5]

John introduces us to some *religious* people with this devilish kind of faith: "Many even among the leaders believed in him. But because of the Pharisees they would not confess their faith for fear they would be put out of the synagogue; for they loved praise from men more than praise from God."[6]

In other words, these leaders were intellectually aware that Jesus was of God. But they refused to put the kind of *trust* in Him that leads to a vibrant relationship with God.

For John, faith is always a verb. Faith is action. So we do not find faith by sitting in an ivory tower examining theoretical arguments. No! Faith gets out in the dusty streets of life and lives by what God says. As we do that, piece by piece, God's will makes more and more sense. And the longer we live it, the stronger we believe it.

Now, you might say that this emphasis on action detracts from faith. Aren't we supposed to trust in Him instead of taking matters into our own hands?

Look at it this way:

I go to my doctor when I am sick because I trust him. But suppose he jots down a prescription and orders, "Take one a day for a week." Next week I come back complaining that I feel sicker than I did last week.

The doctor inquires, "Did you take the medicine?"

"Well, no, Doc. If I were to take those pills, I might leave the wrong impression. It is *you* I trust, not the pills or the pharmacist or my ability to buy pills."

The doctor might say, "Either take the pills or get another doctor. If you trust me, you will take my medicine." In other words, "Trust me and then *act* on what I tell you."

Or as Jesus put it, "If anyone chooses to do God's will, he will find out whether my teaching comes from God or whether I speak on my own."[7]

FAITH FITS

To do what faith would do leads to experiencing what faith experiences. When we do what faith would do, we find out that faith fits. The living Word becomes self-validating in an even more concrete way than the "Aha!" experience.

For example, Jesus said, "It is more blessed to give than to receive."[8] "Well," you say, "that is a nice theory—but is it really true?" There is really only one way to find out: *Give!* Give generously and consistently, and before long you will begin to experience the blessings of being a giver. And when that happens you can say, "Hey, I *know* that is true!"

Sharon found out firsthand that the lifestyle of faith fits. A few years ago, Sharon's faith was on hold. She felt that she should contribute more to God's work, but she didn't really feel like it. Besides, she didn't really think that she had anything important to give—or that anyone would want her "gift." Sharon did want more faith, however. So she committed to teach a fourth-grade Sunday-school class.

But there's a little more to this story. Sharon has multiple sclerosis and lives in a wheelchair. Just getting around is a chore in itself. She knew that the hassle of transporting her teaching materials to and from her house, car, and classroom could overwhelm her, but Sharon wanted to do what faith would.

That was several years ago! Today Sharon is a valued member of a strong teaching team. Her kids adore her—and they have learned a lot about handicaps too. Another little serendipity: At this writing, Sharon gets around in a motorized wheelchair that admiring friends gave her. Most important of all, Sharon has found that doing what faith would do "fits." New feelings of self-worth and trust in God's care have blessed her with a vastly improved quality of life.

Bud also discovered that a faith lifestyle fit his deepest realities. At seven o'clock on that early December night, Bud finally steered his Olds 88 out of the office parking garage onto Hastings street, heading toward the freeway and then home to a roaring fireplace, warm dinner, and the family he loved.

But just as Bud eased through the light at Hastings and Grant, he caught a glimpse of a skinny kid who looked about twelve years old. The boy was leaning against the dark red brick of the old Mims building, wearing only ragged sneakers, cutoff jeans, and a soiled T-shirt—not nearly enough clothing for the thirty-eight degree and dropping temperature.

Bud accelerated on past, anxious to get home and glad that the boy was not his problem. But he couldn't dismiss the shivering kid from his thoughts, so at the second cross street he swung a U-turn and headed back toward the Mims building. Bud opened his car door and hollered, "Son, why don't you go on home? It's cold out here."

> Bud discovered that a faith lifestyle fit his deepest realities.

The boy stiffened and retorted, "It's none of your business, mister."

Bud would have liked to have left it there, but something wouldn't let him. He killed the engine and stepped from the car. "Son, I'll make it my business. You can't stay out on a night like this dressed like you are. Go home!"

"I can't go home, mister. See this slip of paper? It's a grocery list. There's a hole in my pocket, and I lost the five-dollar bill Ma gave me with the list. And I can't go home without the groceries, mister."

"Well, just go back and get another five-dollar bill."

"Mister, you don't know my daddy when he's drinkin'. This is Friday night, you know. I just can't go home without the stuff."

Bud fished a crisp bill from his wallet and beamed, "Look here. I've got five dollars just waiting for a boy like you."

"Nope. No way I can pay you back, mister."

"Sure. I've got a few errands that need running tomorrow—about five dollars' worth."

Bud and the boy struck a deal. The money changed hands, and the kid headed across to Safeway. Bud stood on the corner and watched the kid through the big window as the checker packed the groceries in a sack and made change, which the boy stuffed into his pocket. Picking up his sack, he squared his shoulders like a man and headed whistling out the door.

But then the young man spotted Bud and turned into a little boy again. He rushed across, walked up, and put his hand on Bud's chest.

(When Bud told his wife about the incident, as he got to this part his voice choked and tears flooded his eyes.) The kid looked up at Bud. His chin quivered, and he said, "You know what, mister? I sure wish't you was my daddy!"

Bud said later that he drove another thirty blocks, just looking for another kid he could give five dollars to.

Of course, these blessings received through generosity are but one example of doing what faith would do. Scripture is loaded with lifestyle, attitude, and value choices that can only be understood when experienced.

How can I know what the fruits of loving the unlovely feel like until I have loved someone who is unlovely? How can I know the exhilaration of going without a meal or movie in order to feed a homeless family until I have done it? How can I know the confidence of depending on God's care until I have actually taken a risk and stepped out in faith?

We could argue from now until doomsday about whether the "faith walk" fits life and never reach a conclusion. But if you start living the faith, doing what faith would do, like Sharon and Bud, you will see that the message of the faith "fits life"—that it works. So I urge you to begin your experiment of faith; try the "faith theory" out in practice.

FAITH OBEYS

Another word for doing what faith would do is *obedience*—and obedience produces faith. As we continue to walk along the path to faith in obedience to the guidance God gives us through the Bible and other Christians, our experience continues to build our faith.[9]

But the reverse is also true, of course: We cannot be believers if we choose to be disobedient while we are trying to believe. If we simply go on doing our own thing and living outside God's will but still longing for faith to happen—it won't. Disobedience produces doubt.

Disobedience cuts two ways. It can mean refusing to step out in faith, declining to act, neglecting to do something God wills us to do. It can also mean going the wrong way, choosing to do something God has forbidden. When we do that, we take a side road off the path of faith and quickly lose our way.

"Doing what faith would do," then, not only means beginning (or continuing) your journey of faith but correcting your course if necessary—admitting you've gone in the wrong direction and then choosing to get started once more on the right road.

The old-fashioned term for this kind of necessary turnaround is *repentance*. And Jesus made it clear: "Unless you repent, you too will all perish."[10]

A man who served as one of my faith mentors in my early life later left his wife and took the wife of another man, destroying two marriages, wrecking two families, and damaging two churches. Yet he insisted he was "in the center of God's will."

How did he decide that? Well, he was approaching a business deal in which he stood either to make or lose approximately fifty thousand dollars. So he struck a deal with God: "Lord, if it is your will that I live with this woman, confirm that by letting me make this fifty thousand dollars. If this relationship is outside your will, please confirm that by having me lose the fifty thousand." My friend made the fifty thousand and more, so he assumed that it was "clearly God's will that we should live in this relationship."

I see my friend rarely these days. But the last couple of times I talked to him, he was having trouble with his faith. His vocabulary had shifted significantly.

We cannot love God's will while we are walking outside His ways. I predict that my friend will only continue farther into doubt unless he decides to turn from his wrong direction and, in old-fashioned language, "repent and obey." God withdraws insight from a divided heart.

Years ago and far away, a coworker to whom I had felt very close subtly began moving toward more impersonal conversation and slowly distanced himself socially from me. I searched my soul, wondering if I had offended him. Then he began avoiding group devotions, even subtly making light of the need our staff felt for such times. He explained that he was wired differently and "that emotional sort of thing" was not how he got his spiritual batteries charged. He even implied that some of us were imposing our needs on the rest of the group. Self-doubt plagued me. Time revealed, however, that this brother had drifted into the grip of gross immorality. Of course he did not want to be close to his fellow ministers and be open with them, much less approach closer to the gaze of the Holy One.

How can we face God's awesome holiness while we are nurturing a rebellion, whether the sin is scarlet or any other color of the rainbow? Although we may say we long to "find God" while willfully choosing to disobey Him, we would be scared to death if we actually found Him.

Make no mistake about it: Disobedience will always sap our faith. But wonderful release and renewal come through genuine repentance, confession, and forgiveness. Lost faith is regained. Fresh vitality is restored! We're once more on the road of growing faith.

Repentance, like faith itself, is a choice, a decision. As John the Baptist put it, we "repent and believe."[11] And when we do that, then believing causes more repenting, and repenting produces more believing, and we continue in an upward spiral of growing faith. Growing faith walks in the flow of ongoing repentance and returning to the will of God.

The old hymn says it well:

When we walk with the Lord
In the light of His Word,
What a glory He sheds on our way!
While we do His good will,
He abides with us still,
And with all who will trust and obey.
Trust and obey,
For there's no other way
To be happy in Jesus,
But to trust and obey.[12]

MOVING ON IN FAITH

In the past five chapters, I have suggested some practical steps to help you move on toward a stronger and richer life of faith.

1. Decide whether or not you really want to believe.
2. Go where faith is.
3. Clarify the object of your faith.
4. Feed your mind with faith-building material.
5. Do what faith would do.

Actually, these steps walk in a circle and keep returning us to that one key issue: What do you will at the center of your heart? These five steps will not guarantee faith, nor are they all there is to the process of "help for my unbelief." But they can help get us off dead center and moving down the road toward living faith. And the good news is that as we move out toward God with whatever faith we can muster, Jesus comes out to meet us. In fact, as we continue our stumbling journey, He is with us all the way.

That does not matter.
You bring me news
Of a door that opens at the end
Of a corridor, sunlight and singing;
When I had felt sure
That every corridor led to another,
Or to a blank wall; that I keep moving.
—T. S. ELIOT

Dancing on the Rim of Mystery

Aldous Huxley once wrote that human beings are "multiple amphibians"—creatures designed to make our way through many worlds at once: social, spiritual, emotional, cerebral, aesthetic, sexual, psychological, and so forth. But, he added, since the industrial revolution harnessed our energies to production and the technological revolution turned us into information manipulators, we tend to live primarily in the two logical worlds: those of data and productivity. These worlds are crowding out our other worlds, which are thus atrophying. As a result, we are losing touch with what it means to be human.

Sounds accurate to me, Mr. Huxley!

Something like this can happen to faith as well. The rational, informational, and linear-sequential worlds of productivity tend to dominate in our lives these days. Consequently, the rest of our worlds suffer neglect, and we are losing touch with much of what it means to believe.

The mind-set of the times threatens to strip our faith of symbols, rituals, dramas, mystery, poetry, and story, which say about life and God what logic and reason and rationalism can never say. Instead, we attempt to analyze and explain God. *Scripture* becomes

mere religious information and *faith* simply the progressive realization of moral or religious goals.

From this perspective we cannot expect
anything but flatness. One-dimensional
faith, like a tent with only one peg, easily
collapses. Yet we Americans tend to secure
our faith primarily with the one peg of logical thought. Faith that is only cerebral in
content and only goal-oriented in activity
is one-dimensional.

Life is too full of
mystery and majesty
to be reduced to
matters of
information and
production.

There is nothing wrong with trying to understand our faith. But
many of us try too hard. We attempt to explain the unexplainable,
find out the undefinable, ponder over the imponderable, and
unscrew the inscrutable. A life of real, meaningful faith can't be
treated that way. Trying to do so only leaves people with swollen
heads and shrunken hearts.

God is too vast and mysterious to be confined to linear-sequential
thinking and production-oriented activity. That's true of people as
well. There is far more to us than words and mouths and ears and
brains. Life is too full of mystery and majesty to be reduced to matters
of information and production.

When the Australian aborigine is asked the meanings of mysterious paintings on the wall of a sacred cave, he cannot explain them
in words, so he dances his answer! We, too, know very well that
many of life's best valuables defy explanation:

- The explanation of love is not love.
- The explanation of a joke is not humor.
- The explanation of music is not music.
- The explanation of a poem is not poetry.
- And the rational explanation of religion is not the same as
  touching the Holy One!

Who can completely diagram the meaning of my wedding ring?
Or analyze the meaning of flowers brought to a hospital room? Or
explain the bread and the wine of Communion? Sure, you can say

words about them that may well be true, but you can never say quite enough, never convey all the truth.

Henry Van Dyke said of one of his stories, "What does it mean? How can I tell? What does life mean? If the meaning could be put into a sentence there would be no need of telling the story."[1] And when the great ballerina Anna Pavlova was asked, "What do you say when you dance?" she replied, "If I could tell you, I wouldn't need to dance."

Yes, indeed! When we distance our deeper selves from the fine art of believing, we rob ourselves of most of what it means to believe. Real, dynamic faith takes up our dramatic mysteries and gets inside of them, no matter how undramatic, ordinary, or even misshapen we may think our own lives to be. Full faith gets down to the part of us that we cannot explain or quantify but that shapes the direction of our lives.

THE CASE FOR MYSTERY

The Bible will not clear up every doubt. In fact, sometimes Scripture seems, at least at first glance, to generate new doubts. The Bible embraces paradoxes.

For example, the Proverbs say, "Do not answer a fool according to his folly." Then the next verse instructs, "Answer a fool according to his folly."[2] Make up your mind, Solomon! Paul charged, "Carry each other's burdens," then added three verses later, "Each one should carry his own load."[3] Which is right, apostle? Scripture says that Christians are "set...free" and should not be "burdened again by a yoke of slavery," yet at the same time we are to be "slaves to righteousness."[4]

And these are only some of the little paradoxes. There are larger ones as well—predestination and free will, works and grace, judgment and mercy, just to hint at a few. Possibly you know how to explain these. But if you read long enough, you will confront biblical paradoxes that confound the wisdom of the ages. Heaven offers some of her best truth suspended between such paradoxes.

The Word of God also presents mysteries. For example, God

exists. God has all power. God is all-knowing. God is all-loving. But thousands of people starved to death again this year, and the horror of war has slaughtered thousands more. Why? If God knows, why does He not act? If God loves, why is He not moved to do something? Not enough power? Come on, now. Either God is not all-powerful or He is not all-loving or He is not all-knowing or—He doesn't exist!

I believe the living God knows, loves, and is omnipotent. Yet I do not know how to untangle this dilemma. Oh, I have read books on it: C. S. Lewis's *The Problem of Pain* and one chapter of *God in the Dock*, Philip Yancey's *Disappointment with God*, and others. Yet this mystery still boggles my mind. It has boggled the best minds of the centuries.

And yet mystery is precisely the point, isn't it? A God so small that we limited humans can explain Him is not big enough to be worshiped.

Years back, my friend Juan Monroy, a Christian journalist in Madrid, Spain, was among those reporters selected by the Spanish government to interview the American astronaut James Irwin, who was on a European tour after his Apollo 15 mission to the moon. Monroy asked the astronaut, "What did you feel when you stepped out of that capsule and your feet touched the surface of the moon?"

To Monroy's utter surprise, Irwin replied, "It was one of the most profoundly disillusioning moments of my life."

Monroy pressed the astronaut: "How could standing on the moon be so disappointing?"

Irwin explained, "All of my life I have been enchanted by the romance and the mystery of the moon. I sang love songs under the moon. I read poems by moonstruck poets. I embraced my lover in the moonlight. I looked up in wonder at the lunar sphere. But that day when I stepped from the capsule onto the lunar surface and reached down at my feet, I came up with nothing but two handfuls of gray dirt. I cannot describe the loss I felt as the romance and mystery were stripped away. *There will be no more moon in my sky!*"

Monroy observed further, "When we come to the place that we think we comprehend and can explain the Almighty, there will be no more God in our heavens."

God's Word not only *reveals* His endless love and awesome holiness but also *veils* His majesty in mystery and paradox that transcend comprehension. He is God, not human!

"My thoughts are not your thoughts," says the Lord, "neither are your ways my ways."[5] I think God is also saying, "And you, my children, are not just mortal either. You will always be stretching beyond your temporary finitude, watching for glimpses and listening for whispers from infinity."

God has put eternity in our hearts. A part of us lives in worlds beyond, even if we at times find it difficult to stay in touch!

Oh yes! Because both God and humanity are too big for explanation, the Bible conveys far more than information and logical objectives. God speaks to all of our worlds through drama, music, poetry, stories, paradox, and mystery. The Bible teases out nuances that stretch far beyond mere data in ways too wonderful to explain and too sacred to be contrived. Full faith awakens all of our worlds and dances through them, touching us on multiple levels and moving us with profound force. This kind of faith, like a tent pegged from many angles, is much less likely to go flat.

AWAKENING ALL YOUR WORLDS

So, what does all this have to do with handling doubt?

Simply that you can discover—or recover—the salty tang of life and faith, the vigor and potency of believing and, consequently, of really living. You can let God reawaken all the worlds of your being and ever so gently shape out a rich, full faith. To do so, however, you may need to make some changes in the way you approach your life.

First, you may need to slow your pace. It's always tempting to grab hold of faith or to "fix" broken faith in a hurry, because we in our culture are so obsessed with speed and productivity. But in our wild attempts to save time, we can easily lose eternity. Faithful living— life that is full of faith—rarely comes in the midst of hastiness. To find our way into faith, we may need to lower the RPMs and cool our engines.

Second, you may need to still the noise and search for solitude so that you can listen for God's voice. Elijah, who listened for God's voice in a mighty wind and in an earthquake and in a raging fire, heard Him only in a "still small voice."[6] In a world saturated with woofers, tweeters, traffic, television, jet whistles, disk jockeys, sirens, and screams, how does a person contemplate the God of the still, small voice?

The psalmist says, "Be still, and know that I am God."[7] Henri Nouwen cautioned, "The word is the instrument of the present world, and silence is the mystery of the future world."[8] Solitude may be difficult to find in our world, but nurturing deep roots of faith demands that we search for silence till we find it. And finding silence calls for specific choices. If I do not attack the clock and the calendar, they will attack me!

Nouwen also calls solitude "the furnace of transformation."[9] To explore our own doubt and faith and to confront the Holy One, we absolutely must escape the superficial chatter of multiple relationships and activities and find large chunks of solitude, even in the midst of hectic and overpopulated days.

> Nurturing deep roots of faith demands that we search for silence till we find it.

Third, to awaken all your worlds, you may also need to simplify and prioritize the intake of your life. We get to life just as the Bible says, through the narrow gate. A full life is not reached via the broad way, which seeks to accumulate as many things, ideas, and experiences as possible. Too much will smother us.

Novelist Thomas Wolfe, eager for full life, once said that he wanted "to ride in all the trains, read all the books, and sleep in all the beds."[10] I can understand Wolfe's feelings. I, too, am incurably curious and tend to draw myself into constant overcommitment lest I miss something.

But I am learning that at this pace I do not exhaust events; they exhaust me. Vitality consists in quality of life, not merely in quantity. Eternal life is life that lasts forever. But that truth does not tell the whole story. An eternity of low-quality life would be a curse, not a blessing.

Actually, the biblical concept of "eternal life," when Scripture is taken all together, has as much to do with how well we live as it does with how long![11] Perhaps this is why Francis of Assisi advised:

If you want to live life free,
Take your time, go slowly,
Do few things, but do them well,
Heart-felt joys are Holy.[12]

Fourth, to keep in touch with all that you are and all that God is, you may need to become more reflective. Scripture reminds us that the really blessed people meditate day and night and are like trees planted by the river, drinking up nourishment and life. Rich faith doesn't stop at the surface level. It is planted in fertile soil and draws life from the deep places. The psalmist goes on to indicate that those who don't dig in and go deep get pushed around a lot. They are at the mercy of their environment—"like chaff that the wind drives away."[13]

The deepest of meaning and vitality are found in the mystery of things, even the smallest and most commonplace. We need eyes that see and ears that hear...because down under the surface, beneath what we have always seen and heard and always expect to see and hear, run deeper meanings and realities waiting to be tapped. Says Samuel Miller,

We need to cast away our precious securities, in order to see what is happening for the first time at a new level, with all the fresh vigor of creation's first morning.... Creation is still a reality, but only when we are able and willing to stand face-to-face with its disturbing mystery. It is a mystery that constitutes the climate for believing, and without the mystery any faith is a bore.[14]

Dare to reflect! Settle down beside the drama, the poetry, the mystery of whatever faith we have. Reflect on the tough stuff too. How do you handle pain, boredom, sickness, tragedy, death, life, birth, and nature? This will wake up your slumbering self at levels that can be reached in no other way. Don't be afraid to do this! The Christian faith looks further into what life means than most casual observers see at first glance.

So don't stand back. Come inside the faith. Take that daring leap of faith. Like swimmers in the tide, rather than fighting the forces around us, we need to feel for the current and relax ourselves into its flow. Don't fight faith. Don't merely analyze it. Revel in it. In Him! He won't let you drown.

If you have never had faith, you can learn to believe.

If your faith has gone flat, it can be freshened.

Sure, it may require new habits of thought, new disciplines, new direction. And, of course, it demands a choice that you make and keep on making. But the miracle is not your own ability to be reborn but the unlimited grace available to you. Hope may be just beyond your first step.

You can believe! Faith can be found—and renewed!

I know.

Firsthand.

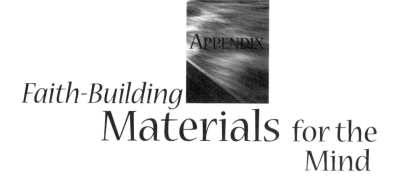

APPENDIX

Faith-Building Materials for the Mind

POPULAR BOOKS

Baxter, Batsell Barrett. *I Believe Because....* Grand Rapids: Baker, 1971.

Green, Michael. *It's a Runaway World.* Downers Grove, Ill.: InterVarsity, 1969.

Johnson, David and Jeff VanVonderen. *The Subtle Power of Spiritual Abuse.* Minneapolis: Bethany, 1991.

Lewis, C. S. *The Chronicles of Narnia.* 7 volumes. New York: Macmillan, 1950–56, 1988.

McDowell, Josh. *More Than a Carpenter.* Wheaton, Ill.: Tyndale, 1987.

_____. *Evidence That Demands a Verdict.* San Bernardino, Calif.: Here's Life, 1993.

_____. *More Evidence That Demands a Verdict.* Wheaton, Ill.: Tyndale, 1975.

Strobel, Lee. *The Case for Christ.* Zondervan, 1998.

_____. *The Case for Faith.* Zondervan, 2000.

VanVonderen, Jeff. *Tired of Trying to Measure Up.* Minneapolis: Bethany, 1989.

INTERMEDIATE BOOKS

Arterburn, Stephen. *The Angry Man*. Dallas: Word, 1991.

Arterburn, Stephen and Jack Felton. *Toxic Faith*. Nashville: Oliver-Nelson, 1991.

Buechner, Frederick. *The Magnificent Defeat*. San Francisco: Harper & Row, 1985.

Campolo, Anthony. *A Reasonable Faith*. Dallas: Word, 1983.

Crabb, Larry. *Inside Out*. Colorado Springs: Navpress, 1988.

Fowler, James W. *Stages of Faith*. San Francisco: Harper & Row, 1995.

Fowler, James W. and Robin W. Lovin. *Trajectories in Faith*. Nashville: Abingdon, 1980.

Lewis, C. S. *God in the Dock*. Grand Rapids: Eerdmans, 1994.

Lewis, David, Carley Dodd, and Darryl Tippens. *Shattering the Silence*. Nashville: Christian Communications, 1989.

Lightfoot, Neil. *How We Got the Bible*. Grand Rapids: Baker, 1988.

Missildine, W. Hugh. *Your Inner Child of the Past*. New York: Simon & Schuster, 1963.

Montgomery, John. *God's Inerrant Word*. Minneapolis: Bethany, 1974.

Palmer, Earl F. *In Search of a Faith That Works*. Ventura, Calif.: Regal, 1985.

Peck, M. Scott. *People of the Lie*. New York: Simon & Schuster, 1997.

_____. *The Road Less Traveled*. New York: Simon & Schuster, 1998.

Phillips, J. B. *The Ring of Truth*. Wheaton, Ill.: Harold Shaw, 1977.

Schaeffer, Francis. *Escape from Reason*. Downers Grove, Ill.: InterVarsity, 1977.

_____. *He Is There and He Is Not Silent*. Wheaton, Ill.: Tyndale, 1980.

Shelly, Rubel. *Prepare to Answer*. Grand Rapids: Baker, 1990.

Shoemaker, Sam. *Extraordinary Living for Ordinary Men*. Grand Rapids: Zondervan, 1965.

Smalley, Gary and John Trent. *The Blessing*. Dallas: Word, 1989.

Taylor, Daniel. *The Myth of Certainty*. Waco, Tex.: Word, 1986.

Tillich, Paul. *Dynamics of Faith*. New York: Harpercollins, 1986.

Vos, Howard F. *Can I Trust the Bible?* Chicago: Moody, 1971.

Walker, Scott. *Where the Rivers Flow*. Waco, Tex.: Word, 1986.

Westerhoff, John. *Will Our Children Have Faith?* Denver: Living the Good News, 2000.

Westerman, Claus. *The Genesis Account of Creation*. Philadelphia: Fortress, 1976.

Yancey, Philip. *Disappointment with God*. Grand Rapids: Zondervan, 1997.

Advanced Books

Guinness, Os. *The Dust of Death*. Westchester, Ill.: Crossway, 1994.

_____. *In Two Minds*. Downers Grove, Ill.: InterVarsity, 1976.

Lewis, C. S. *Mere Christianity*. New York: Touchstone, 1996.

_____. *Christian Reflections*. Grand Rapids: Eerdmans, 1994.

Machen, J. Gresham. *Christianity and Liberalism*. Grand Rapids: Eerdmans, 1923.

Schaeffer, Francis. *The God Who Is There*. Downers Grove, Ill.: InterVarsity Press, 1998.

Young, Edward J. *Thy Word Is Truth*. Carlisle, Pa.: Banner of Truth, 1990.

Tape Resources

Anderson, Lynn. *How to Find Faith*. One tape. Order from Highland Church Cassette Ministry, 425 Highland, Abilene, TX 79605.

Clayton, John N. *Does God Exist?* Six tapes and study guides, Order from John N. Clayton, c/o Church of Christ, 718 E. Donmoyer Ave., South Bend, IN 46614. (219) 291-6852. (John Clayton is a scientist and former atheist.)

Hybels, Bill. *Alternatives to Christianity.* Three tapes. Order from Seeds Tape Ministry, Willow Creek Community Church, 67 E. Algonquin Road, South Barrington, IL 60010. (847) 765-5000.

_____. *Changing Times.* Six tapes. Order from Seeds Tape Ministry, Willow Creek Community Church, 67 E. Algonquin Road, South Barrington, IL 60010. (847) 765-5000.

MacArthur, John. *Nourishment for New Life.* Six tapes. Order from Word of Grace Communications, P. O. Box 4000, Panorama City, CA 91412. (800) 55-GRACE.

_____. *Is the Bible Reliable?* Twelve tapes, two volumes. Order from Word of Grace Communications, P. O. Box 4000, Panorama City, CA 91412. (800) 55-GRACE.

Resner, Andre. *Grief and Faith: Three Profiles of Struggle in the Face of Loss.* One tape, Annual Lectures (April 19, 1989), Pepperdine University. Order from Pepperdine University, Malibu, CA 90605.

Rose, Ron. *Unlocking the Doors of Hope.* Three tapes. Order from Faith in Families Ministry, 5001 Surrey Court, North Richland Hills, TX 76180. (817) 581-3747.

Saunders, Landon. *Exuberance.* Three tapes. Order from Highland Church Cassette Ministry, 425 Highland, Abilene, TX 79605.

_____. *Feeling Good about Yourself.* Four tapes. Order from Highland Church Cassette Ministry, 425 Highland, Abilene, TX 79605.

Strobel, Lee. *Believing the Unbelievable.* Three tapes. Order from Seeds Tape Ministry, Willow Creek Community Church, 67 E. Algonquin Road, South Barrington, IL 60010. (847) 765-5000.

Discussion Questions

Chapter 1–When Faith Goes Flat

1. Who do you know with an authentic faith?

2. What gives his or her faith its authenticity?

3. What experiences have you had when God was especially real to you?

4. What experiences have created doubts?

5. How would you distinguish between a doubter and a non-believer?

6. Where would you place yourself on a scale of 1 to 10, with 1 representing very few doubts and 10 representing unbelief? Why did you give yourself this ranking?

7. Do your doubts affect your relationship with other believers? If so, in what way?

Journal Exercise: In fairly broad strokes, write the story of your faith journey, with attention to experiences that have either built faith or created doubts.

Chapter 2–Tracing Your Tracks

1. Would you describe yourself as a congenital doubter? Why or why not?

2. Of the four basic temperaments, which do you think characterizes you best and how does this temperament play into your experiences of faith and/or doubt?

3. How do your emotions affect your faith? How would you distinguish between an emotional low and a lack of faith?

4. In what way have your faith and/or doubts been impacted by your stage in life?

5. Consider your relationship to contemporary culture—how does the culture influence your faith or add to your doubts?

6. Do you regard your doubt as a spiritual issue? Is it more likely "harm from below" or "help from above"?

Journal Exercise: Reflect on Dean's prayer (p. 28). Write about a crisis you have faced and how you related to God in that crisis. Would you relate to God differently in a crisis at this point in your life?

Chapter 3–Blind Alleys: How Faith Does Not Come

1. Have you faced your doubts with integrity? Have you swept any troubling questions under the rug? Why?

2. Why does "waiting for faith" usually not lead to fewer doubts and a stronger faith?

3. The author defines faith as "a decision of the heart and will to entrust ourselves to God." Is there anything you would add to or change about this definition?

4. Evaluate the statement that "conclusive proof [of God] in the form of rational argument is simply not available." What implications does this have for your definition of faith?

5. If the choice were yours, what would you prefer: conclusive proof of God or an intimate relationship with him? Explain your answer.

6. What evidence of God do you find to be most compelling and encouraging to your faith?

7. Do you think observing a miracle would strengthen your faith? Why or why not?

Journal Exercise: Imagine that God manifested Himself to you in an undeniable way. He says He just wants to talk. Describe how you think the conversation would proceed.

CHAPTER 4—WHAT FAITH IS NOT

1. What role do feelings play in your faith? Have you ever mistaken feelings for the substance of faith?

2. Are you willing to trust in Someone you can't see? Why or why not?

3. When are you tempted to equate faith with religious performance?

4. Is your faith more like a noun or a verb? Explain your answer.

5. How do you respond when you discover an error in your doctrine or understanding of God?

6. Have you ever manipulated or been manipulated in the name of faith? What impact did this have on your faith?

7. How might your doubts spur you on to grow in your faith?

Journal Exercise: Read the quotation by Madeleine L'Engle at the beginning of the chapter. Write a description of God for someone who has never heard of Him. Now write a letter to God. Which was easier? Are you more drawn to the idea of God or to God Himself?

CHAPTER 5—WHAT FAITH IS: A WALKING DEFINITION

1. With whom have you shared your doubts in the past? How did he or she respond?

2. What encourages you most about Abraham's example of faith?

3. Consider the questions that Job and Jeremiah raised to God. If there were one question you could ask God, what would it be? What answer do you think He might give?

4. To this point, has your definition of faith included "struggling with God"? Why or why not?

5. If faith is understood as a journey taken one step at a time, what is the next step you need to take in your journey of faith?

6. As you reflect on your faith and your doubt, what role has your will played in the relationship of the two?

7. What makes it difficult to surrender your will to God? (Be specific.)

Journal Exercise: Read Genesis 12–25. Write about how your faith journey is similar to Abraham's and reflect on what God is teaching you through Abraham's example of faith.

Chapter 6–Stages of the Journey

1. What is one unique aspect of your faith?

2. Are you at one or more of the levels of faith? Which level characterizes your faith most accurately and why?

3. One characteristic of owned faith is a degree of comfort with ambiguity and mystery. How would you illustrate this?

4. Have you ever experienced the silence or distance of God? What resulted from this experience?

5. What is the relationship of freedom to authentic faith? What happens when freedom is sacrificed in the name of faith?

6. Are you more motivated by the praise of men or the praise of God? Would the people who know you best agree with your answer?

7. Why does mature, owned faith continue searching?

Journal Exercise: Write about your search for God. When have you faced opposition and how have you responded? How will you know when you have found God?

Chapter 7–A Will to Believe

1. What are the main reasons you want to believe God? If you don't want to believe, what is holding you back?

2. What impact do pride, career, relationships, and/or social pressure have on your faith?

3. What fears affect the level of your faith commitment?

4. How did your family contribute to a healthy or unhealthy view of God?

5. If you grew up in a church family, in what ways did your church enrich or detract from your faith in God.

6. What ideas about God do you hold that might need to be challenged, changed, or refined?

7. How do we discover what is "hidden in our hearts" that may be distorting our view of God or limiting our faith in Him?

8. What would you say is the main thing that holds you back in your walk with God?

Journal Exercise: Write honestly about your deepest desires, then reflect on how those desires lead you either to or away from faith in God.

Chapter 8–Touching Faith

1. Describe your environment in relation to your faith. Does it function more to nourish or erode your faith?

2. Who encourages you in your faith? What could you do to strengthen your relationship with this person?

3. Why is it so important to be involved in a group of "vibrantly believing people"?

4. How might even the liabilities of your church serve to strengthen your faith?

5. Think of someone you know who is struggling with their faith—what could you do to be an encouragement to them?

Journal Exercise: Write about the church of your youth, the people in that church who impacted you (positively or negatively), and the ways that your faith was nurtured and/or hindered as you matured in that setting. If you did not grow up in the church, write about your impressions of church as a child/young adult and how those impressions influenced you.

CHAPTER 9–TARGETING FAITH

1. How does a person know that the object of his or her faith is the living God?

2. In what ways does your view of God tend to get distorted? What do you do to keep a clear view of God?

3. What aspect of Jesus and His ministry is most compelling to you? What is most troubling?

4. Is it more difficult for you to believe that Jesus was fully human or fully divine? Explain.

5. How does your belief in the humanity and divinity of Jesus impact your view of God?

6. If it is true that "everyone has a crutch," what would yours be and why?

7. If you had no doubt that God knows you by name and loves you dearly, how would your life be different?

Journal Exercise: Write the story of Jesus' life on earth. How does this story change your perspective on what is important in life?

CHAPTER 10–FEEDING FAITH

1. What doubt-building material is part of your mental diet and how is it affecting you?

2. What are some of the resources that have built your faith?

3. Describe an "aha" experience that you have had as a result of your study of Scripture.

4. What role does prayer play in your faith? In what ways are you attempting to listen for God's voice?

5. What parts of your daily or weekly schedule would be conducive to times of transportable solitude?

Journal Exercise: Take some time each day for a week to read God's Word, listen to God, and pray. Each day, write about what you read, what you hear, and what you say to God. At the end of the week, look back through what you have written. What did you learn? How did this exercise affect the rest of your week?

CHAPTER 11–DOING FAITH

1. If you were to begin an experiment of faith, what hypothesis would you want to test?

2. What evidence would an observer find to indicate that you are a disciple or "following learner" of Jesus?

3. Why must faith be more than intellectual assent?

4. In what ways are you acting on your faith?

5. What are the two sides of disobedience, and how does each side undermine faith?

6. Have you ever refused to step out in faith? What happened?

7. Why does repentance restore vitality to faith?

8. How would you describe the "faith lifestyle" that would fit with your "deepest realities"?

Journal Exercise: Based on what you have read in this book, write your definition of Christian faith. Now write out your personal plan for "moving on in the faith."

NOTES

PROLOGUE

1. Mark 9:24, my paraphrase.

CHAPTER 1

1. Gordon Lightfoot, "If You Could Read My Mind," copyright 1969 Early Morning Music. Used by permission.

2. Joseph H. Gilmore (1834–1918), "He Leadeth Me! O Blessed Tho't!"

3. J. Wallace Hamilton, *Who Goes There?* (Westwood, N.J.: Revell, 1958), 18.

4. William Blake, *The Marriage of Heaven and Hell* (Coral Gables, Fla.: University of Miami Press, 1963), 130.

5. Philip Yancey, *Disappointment with God* (Grand Rapids: Zondervan, 1988).

6. Albert Camus, *Caligua*, quoted in William C. Kerley, "Finding Faith Again," *Mission*, November 1972, 6.

7. Os Guinness, *In Two Minds* (Downers Grove, Ill.: InterVarsity Press, 1976), 61.

CHAPTER 2

1. Bernice Neugarten, quoted in Richard P. Olson, "Mid-Life: A Time to Discover, a Time to Decide" (Valley Forge, Pa.: Judson, 1980), 19.

2. John 20:24–28.

3. "God and the American People: 95% Today Are 'Believers'," PRRC *Emerging Trends*, newsletter published by Princeton Religion Research Center, vol. 7, no. 6 (June 1985), 1.

4. Henri J. Nouwen, *Reaching Out* (New York: Doubleday, 1957), 127.

5. Ibid., 128.

CHAPTER 3

1. Tony Campolo, A *Reasonable Faith* (Waco, Tex.: Word, 1983), 18.

2. John 14:6.

3. See John 6:44; Romans 8:28–30; 10:17; 12:3; Ephesians 1:3–14.

4. Joshua 24:14–15; Mark 1:15; John 3:36; Acts 2:40; 7:51; Romans 6; 2 Corinthians 5:1; 2 Peter 3:9.

5. Matthew 11:28, emphasis mine.

6. From *Cow People* by Frank Dobie, copyright 1964 by J. Frank Dobie. By permission of Little, Brown and Company.

7. Frederick Buechner, *Now and Then* (San Francisco: Harper, 1983), 95.

8. Roy P. Basler, ed., *Collected Works of Abraham Lincoln* (New Brunswick, N.J.: Rutgers University Press, 1953), vol. 7, 514–15.

9. Dan Anders, "Life without Faith," sermon delivered at and published by Central Church of Christ, Houston, Tex., February 1971, 3.

10. 2 Corinthians 5:7.

11. Frederick Buechner, *The Magnificent Defeat* (New York: Seabury, 1983), 47.

12. Romans 5:1.

13. Philippians 3:10.
14. John 7:17, emphasis mine.
15. Joshua 24:15.
16. John 12:37, emphasis mine.
17. John 12:39, emphasis mine.

CHAPTER 4

1. Hebrews 11:6.
2. John 8:24.
3. See Romans 1:20.
4. Stephen Arterburn and Jack Felton, *Toxic Faith* (Nashville: OliverNelson, 1991), 136–37.
5. Hebrews 11:1, emphasis mine.
6. 2 Corinthians 5:7.
7. Romans 7:15, 18–19, 24.
8. Romans 3:10; see also Psalm 14:3.
9. Ephesians 2:8.
10. Romans 6:1–2.
11. Mark 1:15.
12. James Gustafson, quoted in *Christian Century*, July 30, 1980, 12.
13. Exodus 20:7 KJV.
14. Os Guinness, *In Two Minds* (Downers Grove, Ill.: Intervarsity, 1976), 28.
15. Ibid.
16. Ibid.

CHAPTER 5

1. Romans 3:23.
2. Romans 2:12.
3. Genesis 12:1, 4, emphasis mine.
4. Genesis 17:16.
5. Genesis 17:17.
6. See Genesis 16:1–7.
7. See Genesis 12:10–20.

8. Genesis 12:12–13.

9. Genesis 12:18.

10. Hebrews 11:10.

11. Hebrews 11:13.

12. Hebrews 11:39.

13. Job 13:3.

14. Philip Yancey, *Disappointment with God* (Grand Rapids: Zondervan, 1988), 233.

15. Jeremiah 12:1.

16. Luke 7:19.

17. Earl Palmer, *A Faith That Works* (Ventura, Calif.: Regal, 1985), 106.

18. Matthew 27:46.

19. Andre Resner, *Grief and Faith: Three Profiles of Struggle in the Face of Loss*, Annual Lectures (April 19, 1989), Pepperdine University, Malibu, California.

20. Genesis 15:6; see also Romans 4:9, 22.

21. Revelation 22:17.

22. "Keep On Walkin'," written by Steve and Annie Chapman. Copyright 1976 Monk and Tid Music. Exclusive adm. by LCS Music Group, Inc., P.O. Box 815129, Dallas, TX 75381. Intl. Copyright Secured. All Rights Reserved. Used By Permission.

CHAPTER 6

1. 1 Peter 2:2, emphasis mine.

2. 2 Thessalonians 1:3, emphasis mine.

3. James W. Fowler, *Stages of Faith* (San Francisco: Harper, 1981); Erik H. Erikson, *Childhood and Society* (New York: Norton, 1950); Janet Hagberg and Robert A. Guelich, *The Critical Journey* (Dallas: Word, 1989); Sharon Parks, *The Critical Years* (San Francisco: Harper, 1986).

4. John Westerhoff, *Will Our Children Have Faith?* (New York: Seabury, 1976), 89–101.

5. Ibid., 91.

6. Hebrews 5:12–14, emphasis mine.

7. Acts 17:11.

8. James 1:6–8.

9. Lois A. Cheney, *God Is No Fool* (Nashville: Abingdon, 1969), 92, emphasis mine.

10. 2 Timothy 3:7.

11. Peter Benson and Carolyn H. Eklin, *Effective Christian Education: A National Study of Protestant Congregations—A Summary Report on Faith, Loyalty, and Congregational Life* (Minneapolis: Search Institute, 1990), as quoted in Eugene C. Roehlkepartain, "What Makes Faith Mature?" *Christian Century*, May 9, 1990, 498.

12. See Galatians 2:3–5.

13. See Galatians 5:1–19.

14. Galatians 3:28.

15. Roehlkepartain, "What Makes Faith Mature?" 498.

16. 2 Timothy 1:12.

17. Stephen Crane, "The Wayfarer," *The Poems of Stephen Crane* (New York: Cooper Square Publishers, 1966), 94.

18. John 5:44, emphasis mine.

19. Earle Nighingale, "Keep an Open Mind," Insight Tape #74 (Chicago: Nighingale-Conant, n.d.).

20. M. Louise Haskins, "The Gate of the Year," in *Treasury of Religious Verse*, ed. Donald T. Kauffman (Westwood, N.J.: Revell, 1947), 99.

PART 4: INTRODUCTION

1. Sam Shoemaker, *Extraordinary Living for Ordinary Men* (Grand Rapids, Mich.: Zondervan, 1965).

CHAPTER 7

1. Quoted in James Robert Ross, "Why I Believe," *Mission*, September 1972, 15.

2. Os Guiness, *In Two Minds* (Downers Grove, Ill.: InterVarsity, 1976), 67–180.

3. Matthew 5:3.

4. Matthew 16:24.

5. David Lewis, Carley Dodd, and Darryl Tippens, *Shattering the Silence* (Nashville: Christian Communications, 1989), 54.

6. Ibid., 53–55.

7. William C. Kerley, "Finding Faith Again," *Mission*, November 1972, 6.

8. Martin E. Marty, *Context*, vol. 23, no. 12 (June 15, 1991), 1–2.

9. Helmut Thielicke, *How to Believe Again* (Philadelphia: Fortress, 1972), 17.

10. John 7:17.

11. See appendix for full bibliographical information on these books.

CHAPTER 8

1. Stephen Arterburn and Jack Felton, *Toxic Faith* (Nashville: Oliver-Nelson, 1991), 283.

2. James 5:16.

3. Eugene C. Roehlkepartain, "What Makes Faith Mature?" *Christian Century*, May 9, 1990, 497.

4. John Westerhoff, *Will Our Children Have Faith?* (New York: Seabury, 1976), 23.

CHAPTER 9

1. Stephen Arterburn and Jack Felton, *Toxic Faith*, (Nashville: OliverNelson, 1991), 297.

2. Dan Anders, "Life without Faith," sermon delivered at and published by Central Church of Christ, Houston, Tex., February 1971, 3.

3. Arterburn and Felton, *Toxic Faith*, 296.

4. John 20:31, emphasis mine.

5. William Melmoth, "To the Emperor of Trajan," *Pliny Letters* (Cambridge, Mass.: Harvard University Press, 1963), book 10, section 96, 401.

6. Quoted from *The Annals of Tacitus*, XV.44 in Philip Schaff, *The History of the Christian Church* (Grand Rapids: Eerdmans, 1910), vol. 1, 387.

7. Luke 3:1.

8. William Whiston, tr., *The Life and Works of Flavius Josephus* (New York: Holt, Rinehart and Winston, n.d.), 535.

9. John M'Clintock and James Strong, *Cyclopedia of Biblical, Theological, and Ecclesiastical Literature*, vol. 2, 190–91.

10. Albert Schweitzer, *The Quest of the Historical Jesus* (New York: Macmillan, 1961), 6.

11. Luke 1:26–27, emphasis mine.

12. See Matthew 13:54–56.

13. See Luke 3:23–38.

14. John 14:6; 6:35; 8:12; 11:25.

15. Hebrews 4:15.

16. Quoted in Douglas Groothius, "The Shamanized Jesus," *Christianity Today*, April 29, 1991, 23.

17. 1 Corinthians 15:19.

18. Romans 3:23.

19. See 1 John 1:9.

20. Isaiah 53:4–6.

21. Hebrews 4:15.

22. Colossians 1:19–20.

23. Colossians 1:21–23.

24. Frederick Buechner, *Magnificent Defeat* (New York: Seabury, 1983), 47.

25. Author unknown, quoted in J. Wallace Hamilton, *Who Goes There?* (Westwood, N.J.: Revell, 1968), 34.

CHAPTER 10

1. Quoted in J. Wallace Hamilton, *Who Goes There?* (Westwood, N.J.: Revell, 1968), 13.

2. Romans 10:17, NKJV.

3. Romans 10:18–19: "But I say, Have they not heard?... But I say, Did not Israel know?" (KJV); "But I ask: Did they not hear?... Again I ask: Did Israel not understand?" (NIV).

4. Hebrews 4:12.

5. John 3:16.

6. Bill Hybels, *Too Busy Not to Pray* (Downers Grove, Ill.: InterVarsity, 1988), 74.

7. John 7:37–39; 14:16–18; Romans 8:9, 14–17; Galatians 5:16–26; Ephesians 6:18, emphasis mine.

8. See 2 Corinthians 12:8–9, my paraphrase.

9. Examples: Matthew 17:20; 18:19; 1 John 5:14–15.

10. Katharina von Schlegel, "Be Still, My Soul," (1752) tr. Jane L. Borthwick (1855).

11. His books include *The Way of the Heart* (New York: Ballantine, 1981), *With Open Hands* (New York: Ballantine, 1981), *Reaching Out* (New York: Doubleday, 1986), *Making All Things New: An Invitation to the Spiritual Life* (San Francisco: Harper, 1981), *In the Name of Jesus: Reflections on Christian Leadership in the Future* (New York: Crossroad, 1989), *The Living Reminder* (Minneapolis, Seabury, 1977), and *Lifesigns* (New York: Doubleday, 1986).

12. Tony Campolo, *The Success Fantasy* (Wheaton, Ill.: Victor, 1980), 52–53.

CHAPTER 11

1. John 8:31–32.
2. Genesis 4:1 KJV.
3. 1 Peter 2:3, tense changed to fit context.
4. James 2:18.
5. James 2:19, my paraphrase.
6. John 12:42–43.
7. John 7:17.
8. Acts 20:35.
9. See John 7:17.
10. Luke 13:3.
11. Mark 1:15.
12. John H. Sammis (1846–1919), "Trust and Obey."

EPILOGUE

1. Henry Van Dyke, *The Story of the Other Wise Man*, preface to the 1923 edition (New York: Grossett & Dunlap, 1923), xv.

2. Proverbs 26:4–5.

3. Galatians 6:2, 5.

4. Galatians 5:1; Romans 6:15–22.

5. Isaiah 55:8.

6. 1 Kings 19:11–12 KJV.

7. Psalm 46:10.

8. Henri Nouwen, *The Way of the Heart* (New York: Ballantine, 1981), 34–35.

9. Ibid., 13.

10. Quoted in William C. Kerley, "Finding Faith Again," *Mission*, November 1972, 6.

11. Hints of this appear in John 10:10; 1:4; Romans 8:10–17; Philippians 1:6; 1 John 5:1–12.

12. Francis of Assisi, from the soundtrack from *Brother Sun and Sister Moon*, copyright 1972 Euro International Films S.P.A. Original story and screenplay by Suso Cecchi D'Amico, Kenneth Ross, Lina Wertmuller, Franco Zeffirelli, music by Donovan. Permission requested.

13. Psalm 1:4.

14. Quoted in Kerley, "Finding Faith Again," 6.